HD 39.5 .S73 1996

Steele, Paul

Profitable purchasing
strategies

CRC
LIBRARY

ER COLLEGE
RCE CENTER
Parkway
Sacramento, California 95823

D0635646

Keep
PerClt

3-2408

Profitable Purchasing Strategies

PROFITABLE PURCHASING STRATEGIES

A Manager's Guide for Improving Organizational Competitiveness through the Skills of Purchasing

Paul T Steele and Brian H Court

The McGraw-Hill Companies

London · New York · St Louis · San Francisco · Auckland
Bogotá · Caracas · Lisbon · Madrid · Mexico
Milan · Montreal · New Delhi · Panama · Paris · San Juan
São Paulo · Singapore · Sydney · Tokyo · Toronto

Published by
McGraw-Hill Publishing Company
Shoppenhangers Road, Maidenhead, Berkshire SL6 2QL, England
Telephone: 01628 23432
Fax: 01628 770224

British Library Cataloguing in Publication Data
Steele, Paul
 Profitable Purchasing Strategies:
 A Manager's Guide for Improving Organizational Competitiveness through
the Skills of Purchasing
 I. Title II. Court, Brian
 658.72

  ISBN 0–07–709214–7

Library of Congress Cataloging-in-Publication Data
Steele, Paul
 Profitable purchasing strategies: a manager's guide for improving
organizational competitiveness through the skills of purchasing/Paul T Steele
and Brian H. Court.
  p. cm.
  ISBN 0–07–709214–7 (alk. paper)
  1. Industrial procurement–Management. 2. Purchasing–Management.
3. Strategic planning. I. Court, Brian H. II. Title.
HD39.5.S73   1996
658.7′2–dc20   95–38512
                                                            CIP

McGraw-Hill

A Division of The **McGraw·Hill** Companies

Copyright © 1996 McGraw-Hill International (UK) Limited. All rights
reserved. No part of this publication may be reproduced, stored in a retrieval
system, or transmitted, in any form or by any means, electronic, mechanical,
photocopying, recording or otherwise, without the prior permission of
McGraw-Hill International (UK) Limited.

2345 BL 99876

Typeset by Computape (Pickering) Ltd, North Yorkshire
and printed and bound by Biddles Ltd, Guildford and King's Lynn
Printed on permanent paper in compliance with ISO Standard 9706

Contents

Acknowledgements

It was Isaac Newton who, in response to compliments about his work, said 'I stand on the shoulders of giants'. For us the same holds true. The ideas and concepts described in this book have their origins with many unsung professionals who were and are brave enough to introduce and test new ways of doing business. It is not possible to identify or list all of these but our thanks go out to them all.

However, within the PMMS organization there are many dedicated professionals who over the years have freely shared their experiences and ideas with us. These concepts are now built into our overall approach so that it is no longer possible to be sure who suggested or developed what. To them goes our sincere thanks and the hope that they will regard this book as much theirs as ours.

In a number of areas it has been possible to identify certain of our colleagues who perhaps deserve special recognition for their contribution. We feel that it is appropriate that they should be named. They are:

Terry H Blake FCIPS MIMgt DMS who over a number of years has managed the practical introduction of these techniques into leading-edge companies, and has continually provided us with feedback so that these techniques can be refined and improved.

Alan T Cooley MCIPS for the development of the vulnerability management concept (Chapter 7) and his major contribution to measurement (Chapter 14).

Patrick J Hill BSc PhD for his contribution to the development of the benchmarking technique (Chapter 14).

John Murphy BA MCIPS MIMgt for his original work on the management of monopolies (Chapter 12).

J Neville Parkin BSc for his major contributions in the area of key account management (Chapter 6) and supplier relationships (Chapters 11 and 13).

Richard C Russill BSc PhD MCIPS for the development of the purchasing strategic models (Chapter 2) in collaboration with Brian

Court, and major contributions to vendor improvement (Chapter 8), supplier relationships (Chapter 13), and measurement (Chapter 14).

Paul Smithard LLB MCIPS for the development of the ten(d) to zero technique (Chapter 8).

Steve Thomas BA FCIPS MCIM MIMgt, who in collaboration with Paul Steele was responsible for many of the concepts described in several of the chapters, but particularly Chapter 4 (False assumptions about the process), and Chapter 5 (Supply positioning).

David S Wood BA MCIPS for his contribution in a number of areas, thus providing us with a reasoned and sound basis for some of our ideas.

Mike N Worthington MCIPS Dip M MCIM C DipAF for his contribution to the development of the benchmarking technique (Chapter 14).

Finally a big thank you to all the purchasing executives who have worked with us over the years and who have allowed us to test out and refine many of these concepts.

Our sincere thanks also go to Philip Holmes who has worked tirelessly on the myriad of detail required to bring this book to fruition.

Preface

We are living in an era of ever increasing change and no more so than in the business world itself. Movements in the international patterns of business together with mergers, acquisitions, shutdowns, and the emergence of new companies are demanding a flexible, rapid approach and response from all those involved in commercial activities. Reassessments of the way large corporations conduct their operations are causing fundamental shifts in organizational structure which in turn is impacting throughout the entire supply chain.

This is forcing companies to reconsider the way in which they conduct their purchasing, by many now regarded as one of a few key profit-generating processes within any enterprise. Gone are the days when supply arrangements could be set up as an afterthought and without due consideration of the supply base. Nowadays such an approach is likely to result in lost production, high input costs, and products which are of inferior quality and too late to market—thus severely eroding the competitive edge.

This increasing recognition that an effective purchasing process can play a highly significant role in the fight for corporate survival and prosperity has been reflected in the UK by

- the establishment of professional purchasing representation in the hierarchy of government with advice being rendered at cabinet level
- the introduction of a National Purchasing Index now frequently a reference point for the media
- the award of a Royal Charter to the professional body.

Similar trends can be identified in many other countries.

Once we start to see purchasing as a business process in which many are involved rather than a stand-alone specialized function, we can start to talk the language of business and leave behind those parochial attitudes which so often act as barriers to getting the job done to maximum advantage. Indeed, just describing purchasing in this way will usually help to bring greater understanding and commitment from those in the organization who are outside of the purchasing function itself.

The debate is now less about 'who does what' and more about 'ensuring that all is done well'. At the same time the role of the purchasing professional throughout the revenue purchase portfolio is changing away from solely an administrative 'doing' activity and more to one of providing a consultancy service to the purchasing process.

However, a great deal more remains to be done if enterprises, whatever their size and sector, are to compete in world-wide markets. This book, based on the collective practical experiences of the PMMS Consulting Group, will describe and examine an array of concepts and techniques which can be used by purchasing professionals to deliver the quality of resource management demanded to stay ahead of competition.

It is hoped that those setting out on a mission to upgrade their purchasing processes will find this a stimulating and informative handbook to guide them on their journey.

Paul T Steele   Brian H Court

PMMS Consulting Group
15 Church Road
Lytham
FY8 2EL
England

1

What is purchasing . . . and why should it be strategic?

In many organizations purchasing remains the least understood and most ineffectively managed of all the business processes. Quite apart from the monetary loss and devastating effect on profit forecasts, mistakes can consequently threaten the viability of the enterprise by allowing costs to rise or delaying the introduction of new products into the marketplace, leading in turn to a loss of competitiveness. Yet managements persist with outdated and inappropriate concepts. Why should this be so, and what can be done about it?

It is possible that the fault lies with the purchasing profession itself. Traditionally there has been no body of academic thought which has been able to move the focus of the process away from routine administrative tasks to the area of readily understandable strategic business concepts. The promotion of the function has too often been left to those individuals who have spent their entire careers working within it at the routine operational level. Such individuals often do not have the broad business vision or experience which is necessary to convince and stimulate boards of directors.

Not unnaturally therefore many members of senior management remain unaware of the large potential that exists for high-class purchasing to make significant improvements in the achievement of corporate goals, including major increases in profit and competitiveness. To convince them of the need to change, purchasing professionals must cease to talk only in terms of administrative activity, or the negotiation of better deals, and enter debate in the wider business sense, concentrating on contributing expertise to meet the strategic thrust of the organization.

The setting up since the early 1990s of chairs of purchasing at a number of universities on both sides of the Atlantic will undoubtedly assist in the process of increasing the understanding of senior management. However, there will never be any substitute for those within an organization being able to promote the function in the language of top management. It is hoped that the concepts described later in this book will provide purchasing managers with the means to achieve this end.

Purchasing defined

Part of the problem stems from the lack of a clear definition about the nature and role of purchasing within organizations. The terms purchasing and procurement are used interchangeably and there is often reference to materials management, logistics, etc. It may therefore be helpful to start by clarifying some of these terms and concepts.

For the purposes of this book we shall use the term purchasing in preference to procurement. We have no special reason for this, other than that of convenience, since we believe both to be equally valid. Purchasing may be defined as follows:

The process by which a company (or other organization) contracts with third parties to obtain the goods and services required to fulfil its business objectives in the most timely and cost-effective manner.

In contrast, purchasing, materials management, and logistics are not interchangeable terms. Materials management is used to describe a range of activities, principally purchasing, inventory management, and warehousing. Logistics is usually materials management plus the movement of materials into, through, and out of a company. However, in some instances logistics may exclude purchasing.

The scope of purchasing

It must be clearly understood at the outset that, according to the above definition, effective purchasing should be applied to obtaining all the goods and services that need to be bought in from outside of the company and that there should be no exceptions at all.

In many organizations there is a traditional view that there are certain areas of expenditure where the requirements are too specialist or too technical to be handled with the involvement of purchasing professionals. Examples are computer hardware and software, energy, advertising, recruitment and staff agency services, design services, and capital items/projects where acquisition is left entirely to 'specialists' or 'technicians'.

We oppose such traditional beliefs. Wide experience shows that there is virtually no field of business operation involving the acquisition of goods and services from third parties which cannot benefit substantially from a more professional and considered purchasing approach. To be specific, we would include, for example, advertising, information technology, research and development, agency staff, and capital purchasing. Later chapters will serve to identify the considerable slip in profit potential which can occur if purchasing in these and other areas is left to untrained staff, however well meaning and however well qualified in their own discipline.

By way of example let us expand on just one aspect: capital purchasing. The expenditure on capital projects is frequently very considerable and the negative impact on the business of non-performance can be devastating. McKinsey has shown that, for high-tech projects, the five year profit effect of being on time but 50 per cent over budget is minus 4 per cent per year.[1] However, more significantly, if the project is on budget but six months late, the decrease in profitability is 33 per cent per year.

Many organizations do of course set up special teams to handle projects of this nature. Frequently these teams will include one or more purchasing professionals. However, in many instances, the buyer is placed low down in the organization and is consequently unable to exert a timely and strategic influence. The role is therefore confined to one of placing orders and verifying decisions already taken by others.

In other organizations it is not unusual to find that the established purchasing departments play no part in the setting up and development of capital projects. However, project delays, budget overruns, and underperformance are frequently blamed on suppliers and subcontractors. A survey undertaken by the Chartered Institute of Purchasing and Supply (CIPS)[2] in 1993 showed that 41 per cent of senior management in the construction industry cited the poor performance of subcontractors as a major problem in winning and executing profitable business.[2] Examples of poor performance due to inadequate capital procurement when the purchasing is left to other specialists are legion but just two are mentioned here.

- A private sector company purchased locomotives which, on delivery, were shown to be underpowered for the duty required. That is, they were unable to draw full loads up an incline within the factory. However, the company buying the locomotives had no means of redress because of inadequate drafting of the contract.
- A financial organization subcontracted out a multi-million pound reimbursable cost software development project on the basis of a two

page letter sent by a senior manager to the supplier. The letter asked the supplier to commence work at the agreed daily fee rates but with no reference to control of costs in the future. After the expenditure of £3 million serious problems were then encountered due to escalating costs (uncontrollable fee rate increases) and poor performance (failure to meet agreed targets) for which there was no contractual control or remedy. The company was faced with the prospect of cancelling the contract and starting again with another supplier or making the best of a very unsatisfactory situation.

All of this underlines the crucial importance of effective purchasing in terms of supply planning, contract strategy, supplier selection, and contract drafting. In many organizations these factors are handled by staff who have had no suitable training in purchasing, or contract formulation.

Well-trained purchasing professionals, working closely with their internal client base, can make a very significant contribution to capital projects; this contribution would include the provision of market information, creative sourcing, innovative contractual arrangements, cost analysis and control, skilled negotiation, and the writing of secure contract terms and conditions.

Creating profit in a business

Businesses exist to make a profit (or for non-profit organizations to maximize value and benefit) and meet the sometimes conflicting needs of all of the stakeholders including employees, customers, and the community. Value to the organization is realized as the difference between the benefit of the output (usually sales turnover) and the expenses needed to run the business, which will include, among other factors, the cost of acquiring the goods and services.

This is illustrated in the model in Fig. 1.1, which identifies four processes which add value and thus contribute to profitability (or, in the case of non-profit organizations, maximize output value). These four processes are purchasing, production/operations, marketing, and logistics.

These four processes contribute to corporate profitability in different ways as described below.

The four processes examined

PURCHASING
The role of purchasing is to manage the **input**, the interface with the supply market. That is, to obtain the bought-in goods and services at the

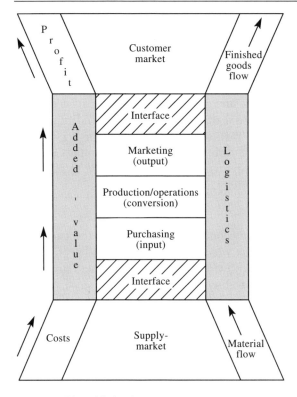

Fig. 1.1   The added-value process

lowest acquisition cost. Lowest acquisition cost can be defined as the provision of the most profitable or cost-effective solution:

- the best purchase price commercially available
- the hidden costs of stockholding and purchasing administration
- the costs of poor quality and late delivery
- the loss of interest on early payments
- subsequent operational and maintenance costs
- the cost of operational failure
- the consequences of a negligent or incapable supplier
- the costs of eventual disposal.

It is important to notice that the purchase price is but one element of the total cost equation and that many other factors must be weighed and evaluated in determining whole life costs and thus the optimum sourcing strategy. Poor input decisions will reduce corporate profitability in direct relation to excess expenditure and may have financial and other consequences well beyond the obvious.

PRODUCTION/OPERATIONS

The role of production or operations is the **conversion** of these 'raw-materials' into saleable goods and services in the most economic manner, making use of the internal resources (personnel and machines) of the organization. Inefficient methods of production or wastage of input materials will again have a direct effect on profitability. Over the years the emphasis on efficiency in this area has been related to facilities-optimization and labour-productivity.

MARKETING

The role of marketing is to create **output** by exchanging the produced goods and services for cash sums which exceed the cost of production. The added-value is created by knowing where the customers are, what they want, and persuading them to buy at the target price.

LOGISTICS

The processes of purchasing, production, and marketing form the core of the way in which a company adds value during the course of its operations. The failure of any one to achieve the optimum will prevent the organization as a whole from reaching its corporate profitability goal.

Logistics operates across all three business processes and can be defined as

The process of managing the flow and storage of an organization's materials from raw-material acquisition to delivery of product to the end customer.

The key logistics activities are given in Fig. 1.2.

Goods inward	Movement of materials from supplier to the organization
Inventory	Stock management against agreed service levels
Warehousing	Storage and handling
Distribution	Movement of materials to meet customer service requirements

Fig. 1.2 Key logistics activities

Logistics can add value in two ways. First, it can reduce operating costs, thus increasing the profit margin. Second, it can give the organization a real or perceived advantage over competitors in terms of customer service levels, thus enabling the organization to achieve higher returns through a differential pricing policy. For example, an organization offering faster response times to meet customers' needs may be able to command a premium price. Ineffective logistics operations will reduce the ability of an organization to realize its profit-potential through either lost market share or reduced margins.

The place of purchasing
Some purchasing professionals will argue that it is entirely appropriate for the purchasing function to be responsible for all associated materials management and logistics activities. While in many businesses purchasing may be assigned these functions, it should be recognized that the activities and skills required for efficient warehousing, inventory management, and materials movement are quite different in nature from those of purchasing.

From a purchasing point of view, matters are made even worse when it is subordinated to a larger materials management or logistics function where the natural tendency is to give insufficient priority to real buying considerations.

Each of the activities within the supply chain needs to be performed at the very highest level of professionalism, contributing to the corporate goals of profitability, customer satisfaction, and long-term growth. While it is fashionable to try to integrate these areas it is important to remember the need for 'functional excellence' in all of them. It will be the choice of the organization, driven by its business needs, to decide whether all functions should be integrated into one supply-chain activity, or whether they should be managed separately.

All four processes are crucial to the success of a business, but it is important to note the different ways in which they influence and make their contribution; therefore, we believe that incorporating purchasing and logistics into one function frequently does a disservice to both. This book will concentrate for the most part on strategies and issues for purchasing to adopt and implement, to enable the function to become a centre of excellence and a major contributor to an organization's profitability and competitiveness.

The financial impact of the functions
Having defined the roles of purchasing, materials management, and logistics it is now appropriate to examine their relative costs and financial impact on the business. Cost responsibility as a percentage of revenue is summarized in Fig. 1.3.

	% of revenue
Purchases for production	50
Purchases for MRO (maintenance, repair and operating supplies)	10
Manufacturing, sales and overheads	30
Profit	10

Fig. 1.3   Typical revenue breakdown

The proportions of Fig. 1.3 represent a simplified model of revenue allocation in a manufacturing company and is derived from data obtained from over one thousand organizations, while Fig. 1.3 indicates that all purchases account for 60 per cent of revenue, it is the case that in some organizations, notably in the defence industry, this figure can approach 80 per cent.

For non-manufacturing and service organizations the numbers will be somewhat different although it is still usual to find that purchasing costs comprise the largest single element of controllable cost. In all industries the trend is upwards as companies decide to contract out more and more of their noncore activity.

Returning to the model in Fig. 1.3, let us assume that the total revenues for a business are £1 million per year. The options to increase profit are

- increase prices
- increase sales
- reduce costs.

Let us now examine how the individual processes and functions can support the drive for increased profitability.

INCREASE PRICES AND SALES: MARKETING

It is the task of marketing to assess whether it is able to raise prices without sacrificing volume, or to increase sales.

The ability to increase prices will be highly dependent on market conditions. If the seller has an unregulated monopoly or has a highly differentiated product then such a move may be possible. A five per cent increase will of course reflect straight through to the bottom line adding £50 000 to the profit. However, the higher that the price moves from the norm, the greater the opportunity for another player to enter the market.

Many market conditions will make it impossible to obtain higher prices without losing market share. An alternative strategy of increasing sales volumes will therefore be considered. Even this may not be possible without trading concessions on price, volume discounts, or other special promotions. However, for the moment, let us consider the effect of increased sales without reduced prices.

If sales are increased by £50 000 (five per cent) there will be a consequent increase in revenue but also in costs. Additional costs will be £25 000 for extra purchased components and raw-materials, together with some proportion of the MRO purchases and manufacturing, sales, and overhead costs. The extent of the latter will be variable depending on the proportions of fixed and variable costs but it would be safe to assume that they would be in the region of £15 000.

This means that for every £50 000 in additional sales there will be an additional cost of £40 000 which leaves a net profit contribution of up to £10 000; the assumption is that there exists a demand for the additional product or that sales could be won from competitors and that price discounting to achieve these would not be required.

REDUCE COSTS: MANUFACTURING (OPERATIONS)
Manufacturing offers the alternative approach of cost reduction. The cost of manufacturing, sales, and overheads (which includes staff and labour costs) together account for 30 per cent of total revenues. Since the late 1960s, a great deal of attention has been focused on reducing costs by increasing staff and labour productivity and decreasing overheads by the rationalization of production facilities. Within these areas very substantial improvements have been made and the scope for further savings may now be severely limited. A five per cent improvement, if it could be achieved, would be worth £15 000, less any costs of implementation, such as redundancy, and productivity payments.

REDUCE COSTS: PURCHASING
As can be seen from the model, the cost of bought-in goods and services is 60 per cent of revenue. A five per cent reduction in the costs of input materials and MRO would result in a saving of £30 000 which would translate immediately into increased profit. Where organizations have undeveloped purchasing functions, a cost improvement of five per cent on purchases is an entirely reasonable objective; this improvement can be achieved with relatively little cost and without distorting the market or changing pricing policies. It is three times that which can be obtained by increasing product sales by five per

cent and more than twice as effective as decreasing other costs by a similar proportion.

Furthermore, a target of five per cent can be regarded as excessively modest. If the entire purchasing process, from inception through to contract performance, is remodelled, then in some instances, savings in excess of 30–40 per cent have been achieved. For non-profit-making organizations, including the public sector bodies which have large purchasing budgets, effective purchasing represents an opportunity to cut costs dramatically or to deliver improved services without additional expenditure.

Better purchasing is not only about lower costs. To confine the view of purchasing to cost reduction only is similar to thinking only in two dimensions. There is a whole additional dimension of additional benefit associated with higher reliability, less production downtime, enhanced quality, faster time to market, and superior environmental performance, to name but a few. These concepts will be dealt with later in this book.

REDUCE COSTS: LOGISTICS

Fig. 1.4 gives an example of total logistics costs expressed as a percentage of revenue. In Fig. 1.3 these are not separately identified as they are spread across purchasing, manufacturing, and overheads.

	%
Transport inwards	1.0
Distribution	4.0
Warehouse costs	3.0
Order processing	1.0
Packaging	2.0
Management	0.2
Stock losses	0.3
Interest on capital	1.0
	12.5

Fig. 1.4 Breakdown of logistics costs

A high-performing logistics function will contribute to corporate profitability by:

- Minimizing the transportation costs associated with the acquisition of purchased goods and services; in this area logistics will need to work

closely with purchasing to ensure that agreements with suppliers offer optimized transport costs.
- Minimizing the quantities of stored purchases, work in progress, and stored finished products while meeting production and customer service levels. In these areas logistics will work closely with production and sales.
- Minimizing the distribution costs associated with the shipment of finished goods to the customer, while meeting agreed service levels. Again, logistics will need to work closely with sales.

All three of these activities—which have a strong element of materials planning—are capable of improvement through techniques such as material resource planning and distribution resource planning. In our model a five per cent reduction in logistics costs would be worth £6250.

SUMMARY ON THE FINANCIAL IMPACT
The financial impact of these various functions on the model can therefore be summarized as shown in Fig. 1.5.

	£	Difficulty
Increase sales prices by 5% without losing volume	50 000	Very high
Increase sales volume by 5%	10 000	Very high
Reduce manufacturing and overhead costs by 5%	15 000	High
Reduce purchase costs by 5%	30 000	Moderate
Reduce logistics costs by 5%	6 250	Moderate

Fig. 1.5 Summary of financial impact

From this it can be seen that all four processes have the capability to make significant improvements to costs and profitability. However, effective purchasing offers the greatest potential for profit improvement and is probably the route which can be followed with least difficulty; it is for this reason that this book will concentrate on purchasing as a means of changing the profit position of organizations.

Purchasing as a strategic process
The previous section has demonstrated the impact that good or bad purchasing can have on costs and profit. If businesses enter into relationships with poor or unproductive suppliers, they will, themselves, operate in an ineffective or unproductive manner.

Since the mid-1970s, this reasoning has led to the conclusion that the true role of purchasing is to manage the supply chain in such a way as to maximize profitability. While undoubtedly this is very important, it is also essential to remember that however good the supply chain, it is in the end dependent on high quality, reliable suppliers. We must ensure that attention to the supply chain does not result in a loss of focus on the suppliers themselves; this would be rather like watering the garden by concentrating on the integrity of a hosepipe while failing to ensure that it is connected to a secure supply of water. Subsequent chapters will explore these ideas in more detail.

For the moment it will be sufficient to reiterate the point that because it can have such a dramatic effect on overall profitability, purchasing demands to be considered as a strategic function. What exactly does this mean and what are the implications for businesses?

World-class purchasing is not about placing orders. The concept of a purchasing department waiting passively until client groups have decided what they need and when they need it is no longer acceptable; this mode of behaviour means that the purchasing contribution—to coin a well known phrase—will be truly 'too little, too late'.

First, a dynamic purchasing department of the future will be involved at every phase of the concept, design, and justification process, influencing specifications and requirements by sharing its up-to-date and in-depth knowledge of the market and the marketplace. It will be persuasive in pointing out the commercial implications of pursuing a particular route or technology.

Second, the function will need to look outward from the business, not only to understand the market as it is today, or might be tomorrow, but also to take actions designed to influence its shape and nature to the benefit of the buying organization. Buyers need to ensure that in pursuing their goals they do not inadvertently change the market to their own disadvantage. For example, the drive to reduce the number of suppliers, commonplace in many organizations, may, in certain markets, reinforce an already existing trend and result in monopoly or limited supply.

It can be argued that this partly falls within the province of supply-chain management but its scope is rather wider than the conventional view. To be really effective, the purchasing function must identify future needs and create new buyer–supplier relationships, and even sponsor new suppliers who are innovative and productive.[3] Objectives such as these will require that management use information about the supply-market as a significant input in all strategic decisions.

The reference to the need for purchasing to be considered as a strategic process, and therefore being considered in corporate strategic decisions, is by no means a new idea. Purchasing literature is littered with a multiplicity of pleas for this to happen. The problem comes when practitioners are asked to define just what is meant by the term 'strategy'.

Purchasing strategy and strategic purchasing

Purchasing strategy and strategic purchasing are terms which are used interchangeably when discussing the purchasing profession and this has led to a certain amount of confusion over exactly what is meant. We have given this considerable thought and have found it helpful to define the terms in the following manner.

Purchasing strategy is concerned with identifying, selecting, and implementing an overall change programme designed to place the purchasing process at the heart of a business so enabling it to make the maximum contribution to corporate profitability while gaining a commercial competitive edge. Among other factors, it encompasses defining the mission of the function, the framework within which to work, and the type of organization and staff which will be employed. It is the foundation on which strategic purchasing is based.

Strategic purchasing is the development of ways of approaching and interacting with the supply-market, taking account of not only the present situation but also how it might develop in the future. It is based on the belief that the buyers can determine and change the supply-market within which they function. Strategic purchasing cannot be applied to the market as a whole but only to specific situations within it. Thus it is possible to have a strategy for the acquisition of such diverse products as printed circuit boards or flour, but not for all commodities treated as one item.

It can be seen from the above that purchasing strategy and strategic purchasing are related and interlocked. Unless a clear purchasing strategy can be set in place, it will not prove possible to undertake effective strategic purchasing. Thus purchasing strategy may be regarded as the foundation stone of strategic purchasing.

Notes and references

1 McKinsey, undated internal report.
2 Garner, E. R. (1993) 'Professional purchasing adds profit', CIPS Report, p. 5.
3 It should be noted that the term 'supplier' has been generally used throughout the text although there will be reference to 'vendors' as well. Supplier may on occasion be another part of the same organization.

2

Building a purchasing strategy

Chapter 1 demonstrated the importance of establishing the appropriate purchasing strategy in creating an effective and forward-looking process. It is therefore important to start with identifying the building blocks of purchasing strategy and defining them for use as the basis for upgrading a purchasing function into a world-class operation. Experience has led to the identification of six building blocks, as shown in Fig. 2.1.

Fig. 2.1 Building blocks of purchasing strategy

For each one it is possible to describe 'best practice' which is based on observations of the situation within leading purchasing organizations, acknowledged as world class, together with a number of concepts which we have seen these organizations use effectively. Descriptions of 'world-class' operation within these building blocks now follow.

Contribution and influence

No matter how professional the purchasing personnel, or how effective their procurement methods, there will be little real impact on the business unless the purchasing function is able to make the kind of high-level contribution which can have an influence on the conduct of the overall business and its future strategy. This building block is concerned with raising the level of contribution and influence to high performance standards.

In raising the profile and influence of the purchasing function improvement steps will include

- raising the seniority of the key personnel
- increasing their ability to contribute to strategic decisions
- extending cross-functional teamworking
- rationalizing and clarifying the authority structures
- increasing the level of involvement with the entire purchasing portfolio
- providing effective and realistic means of self-measurement.

SPECIFIC ISSUES

- The company chief executive will advocate representation of purchasing at board level and, as a result, the senior purchasing executive (SPE) will be established at high level either as a board member or very senior executive reporting to a member of the board. Purchasing will not be part of a wider organization such as materials management or logistics and certainly will not be submerged in a more general services group.
- Purchasing will be regarded by all senior management as a key strategic activity requiring the highest level of professionalism. Evidence of this would be that the SPE participates in corporate discussions which are concerned with profitability, project management, and product development.
- The SPE and the SPE's staff will manage the overall interface between the buying organization and its suppliers, including the behaviour of the user groups. However, there will be a strong emphasis on multi-functional teamwork. The SPE will be seen as a team coach rather than a taskmaster.
- Purchasing's involvement will be in 98 per cent of the organization's spend with suppliers. This means that purchasing will set the policy, influence and monitor activity for this proportion of the spend. Purchasing will be fully involved from an early stage in all major revenue and capital acquisitions; there will be no exceptions on the grounds of being 'too specialist' or 'too technical.'

- The organization will have two clearly defined interleaved types of authority, namely, expenditure and commitment. All authorities will be written down, published, and maintained up-to-date. They clearly take into account any differences arising in corporate policies between capitalized and expenditure moneys.
- The SPE will be delegated complete and unlimited commitment authority by the board, thus balancing the expenditure authority assigned to user management and the payment authority delegated to finance. The SPE will also be authorized to redelegate commitment authority as seems appropriate; such redelegation can be either to other senior line executives or to members of the purchasing department. The SPE retains overall responsibility and is accountable for all purchasing actions whether within the SPE's own centralized department or to other locations in other parts of the organization.
- The organization will have moved away from the use of formal contract committees but the SPE will be charged with ensuring, nevertheless, that all interested parties have had adequate input to and are supportive of the purchasing decisions.
- Purchasing staff will have been given extensive commitment authorities and encouraged to use them to the full. The actual level of authority will be dependent on seniority, experience, and previous performance but will not be modified according to the purchasing method employed.
- There will be considerable evidence of cross-functional teams, of which purchasing is a full member, which are cooperating throughout the entire procurement process from inception to first use and performance review. Via these, purchasing will be making major and significant contributions to corporate strategy.
- Performance measurement will be well developed with the emphasis on corporate contribution. In the most advanced organizations this measurement will be an integral part of the overall management information system and in the very best will be concerned with the quality of the process rather than specific tasks.

Purchasing and audit framework

Experience shows that in many organizations there is either no real control of the purchasing process or it is surrounded by bureaucracy and unworkable regulations which stifle initiative and good purchasing practice.

This building block creates an effective regulatory framework within which the purchasing process is performed; it will include the production and promulgation of a mission or role statement, establishing policy and procedure manuals which are 'user friendly' and allow for a flexibility in approach to the purchasing process, empowering purchasing staff and encouraging them to use their entrepreneurial skills; such a framework would include the provision of adequate controls and the establishing of an effective relationship with the internal audit function.

SPECIFIC ISSUES

- The organization will have created, written, and published a brief **role statement** describing concisely the role of the purchasing function and how it interacts with other departments. There will be a considerable orientation towards the supply-market.
- The purchasing department will have devised and published a brief set of **purchasing policies** in the form of a well-printed slimline booklet. These policies will cover the broad principles to be followed when anyone is undertaking purchasing transactions and would be the basis of any audit. It will have been given wide circulation and most managers will need to be familiar with its contents.
- A statement with regard to ethical behaviour standards will receive prominence in the policies document. Requirements will be laid down in clear unambiguous language and methods will be devised and promulgated to ensure compliance.
- Both the role statement and purchasing policies will be clearly seen to have the full and unqualified endorsement of the board.
- The SPE will have written and published a set of **model purchasing procedures**. Because these may be subject to frequent change—and amendment—they may be in the form of a ring binder and will normally be issued to and held by all those who make significant commitments on behalf of the organization. These are **model procedures**, intended as a guide, as they have been drafted to comply with the purchasing policies.
- Procedures are designed to recognize and respond to both the organization's requirements and the variety of needs in the marketplace, with the objective of obtaining the best commercial outcome. Accordingly, the policies and procedures will be written in such a way as to allow professional buyers to exercise considerable judgement concerning the purchasing methods to be used. Whereas the policies are mandatory, the procedures are for guidance, and other methods may be used provided they comply with the policies. Apart from considerations (such as those contained within the policy framework of EU directives) there will be no inference, for example, that competitive tendering is the preferred or correct method of purchasing, or that all deviations require justification.

- The procedures for the identification, financial approval, and commitment of capital expenditure will be such as to ensure that the buying organization can extract maximum commercial advantage from the marketplace. Outline financial approval will be obtained before the suppliers are asked to quote, thus allowing maximum leverage during bidding and/or negotiation.
- All purchasing transactions will be assigned a unique purchase order number which suppliers will need to quote in all correspondence and communications. For all transactions above a minimum level it will be necessary to issue a standard purchase order using standard forms.
- All purchase orders, other than for certain low value, low risk items, will be accompanied by a set of terms and conditions which will govern the transaction. Where the supplier has long-term contracts or a long-term association, the buyer will have set up a mutually agreed set of terms which will govern all transactions. For large complicated contracts use will be made of contractual forms standard to that industry and modified, as required, by the buying organization. Suppliers' terms and conditions will not be accepted.
- Where contracts of a reimbursable cost nature are let, the buying organization will ensure that they include sufficiently powerful 'right of audit' clauses to ensure that value for money is being achieved.
- For those members of staff who are involved only with small purchases, the purchasing department will issue a brief **user buyer's guide** which may be in the form of a folded A4 sheet or plastic card and which sets out the brief rules that must be followed when purchasing small items.
- Special, very simple, and easily usable procedures will have been designed for low value, low risk transactions although these remain under the nominal control of the SPE; such methods may include very innovative approaches such as charge cards, self-payment, direct debiting, or the elimination of invoices.
- Purchasing will have set up a comprehensive list for controlling approved suppliers. At the one extreme, simple procedures will be in place—independent of purchasing—for ensuring that only 'bona fide' companies and organizations can be made payments. On a more limited basis a **preferred suppliers list** will have been created for key strategic items. The level of qualification will depend on the standard of performance required. However, the list will not be used in such a way as to prevent the identification and use of new suppliers with innovative offerings.
- All purchasing activities will be subject to frequent and detailed audit by an independent internal audit group. The frequency will be related to

past performance; that is, the more satisfactory the outcome, the longer the interval between audits.

- The auditors will be trained in understanding and implementing the principles of fully operational auditing and so be competent to audit the purchasing function. They will concentrate on substantive issues and be less concerned with trivial violations. Where justifiable criticisms are made, the SPE will have agreed and put in hand corrective measures. Senior management will seek follow-up confirmation that the corrective measures have been implemented.
- The purchasing function itself will maintain a system of self-audit, involving the independent auditors particularly where controls advice is required on the development of new purchasing tools.
- This entire framework will be kept under programmed review and modified and updated for changes in circumstances and will monitor— for example—the mandatory implications of EU directives whenever applicable.

Organization

The organizational framework within which the purchasing function operates can have a profound effect on its effectiveness and its relationships with key clients. Underlying the organizational issues is the dichotomy relating to centralization and decentralization. This building block creates an organizational structure based on **Centre-Led Action Network (CLAN)** or an appropriate development of it. Whatever the structure, the levels of internal hierarchy will be few, and a high level of networking between buyers and buying organizations will exist. Methods to balance and allocate workloads will be based on **supply positioning** or similar techniques and there will be a bias towards 'upstream' activities with the eventual elimination of failure-related activities such as expediting, invoice chasing, and quality checking.

SPECIFIC ISSUES

- A fundamental review of organizational structure will have been undertaken with the result that the CLAN approach has been selected (see Chapter 13). If this has been operating for any time, tensions between centre and the decentralized groups will have all but disappeared.
- The organization of the central purchasing department, if one still exists, will contain as few levels of supervision and management as possible, consistent with being able to control the activity.
- Responsibilities will be allocated so as to continuously balance workload and to provide user groups with a single point of contact within

purchasing. Consideration will have been given to the use of supply positioning (see Chapter 5) or equivalent analysis tool as a means of more appropriate allocation.

• Emphasis will be on upstream activity and the upstream/downstream balance (UDB) indicator (see Chapter 3) will be at 70 or above. Certain functions such as expediting and invoice matching and checking will have disappeared, no longer being considered necessary, thus reflecting the development of electronic systems.

• Buyers in different locations will be networking with one another so that the organization as a whole is building up a powerful information and leverage matrix. Job descriptions will reflect the strategic nature of purchasing and will properly reflect the level of responsibility.

• A promotional career path for high quality buyers will be in existence either as part of the overall management development programme or as part of a technical expertise development programme. In the latter, titles such as senior buyer and associate buyer will be used to acknowledge publicly more seniority, and will reflect enhanced responsibilities and remuneration.

• Above all, a culture of trust and personal empowerment will exist, as will the encouragement of considered risk taking, and a learning from failure. This will result in a high level of motivation and personal ownership of the activity together with a unified sense of purpose.

• The organizational structure will be kept under continuous review in order to ensure that it is consistent with the current and future objectives of the company.

Relationships (internal and external)

Purchasing can no longer be considered an isolated function, working at arm's length from suppliers and internal clients alike. The best operators work closely with all parties in the supply chain to achieve an overall goal of competitive edge for the buying organization.

This building block encourages procurement involvement early in the procurement cycle, the effective operation of multi-functional teams, and the management of all of the buying organization's contacts with suppliers. It also focuses on the relationship with suppliers, starting with differentiating between the various types of relationships which are appropriate and this will involve the application of strategies specific to a supplier or group of suppliers as opposed to a uniform approach to the supply-market.

Supplier involvement in design and development will be encouraged for certain key products and a joint approach taken towards enhancements in quality, delivery, and service together with significant reductions in total cost and the implementation of techniques used for measuring and improving supplier performance.

SPECIFIC ISSUES

- There will be a general recognition of the importance of suppliers to the success of the enterprise. This will be evidenced by the time and attention devoted to getting the supply base right. There will not be a blanket target of reducing the number of suppliers by a given proportion or to a given number. The approach will be much more selective with the aim of rationalizing the supply base while, if necessary, increasing the number of suppliers in certain sectors.

- The purchasing department will be using the supply positioning tool (see Chapter 5) or another similar technique, to segment the supply-market to assist in developing strategies *vis-à-vis* certain categories of suppliers and whether their numbers should be increased or decreased.

- Arising from this, one would expect to see a comprehensive supplier relationship programme which identifies a range of relationships selected according to the needs. The identification of areas where supplier partnerships should be developed and where they definitely should not, would be a prominent feature. Discussions with senior managers would reveal a recognition and an understanding of the complexities and pitfalls of setting up supplier partnerships.

- This recognition will also have resulted in efforts to present the buying organization as a preferred customer using the techniques of **procurement marketing** (see Chapter 8). Included in this will be a brief guide for suppliers entitled 'Selling to . . .'.

- Information on key suppliers will be detailed and comprehensive. Wherever possible, independent checks on supplier data will have been made. In addition to information on products and capacity, buyers will have collected information on corporate structure, organizational goals, management expertise, etc.

- Suppliers will be involved in considering detailed options and concepts at an early stage. They will be encouraged to generate ideas to provide as innovative and comprehensive a service and to subscribe to the quality assurance philosophy. Every effort will be made to avoid demarcation between suppliers and between suppliers and the buying organization.

- Supplier performance will be subject to monitoring to enable the buyer to have an overview of how the supplier is performing in terms of quality, price, delivery, after-sales service, reliability, administration, and paperwork, etc. There will be substantial evidence of meaningful actions—including total quality management (TQM) initiatives—taken to improve the performance of key suppliers rather than frequent switching for minor advantage; such action will be in the form of joint cooperative effort combining the knowledge and talents of both buyer and seller.

- Where no suitable suppliers exist, the purchasing function will be developing suitable sources to meet current and future needs, such strategies will include **reverse marketing** initiatives (see Chapter 8).
- Buyers will be in continuous discussion with clients concerning requirements and will be making frequent visits to key suppliers and, consequently, spend a substantial time away from the office.
- Although free contact between visitors from suppliers and the buying organization's personnel is encouraged, it has been made absolutely clear that the purchasing department is ultimately accountable for managing the relationship and that only its staff are authorized to enter into legal commitments. Internal users will have been trained to deal with these visitors consistent with this approach.
- Where other agencies (e.g. government departments) have an interest in the company's procurement activity, then it is purchasing that will have the prime link.

Systems

Computerized systems offer organizations the opportunity to increase dramatically the information on which to base decisions and a means of eliminating routine administrative activity. To be fully effective, organizations must ensure that the needs of the business drive the systems design and operation and not vice versa.

This building block will propose the introduction of computerized purchasing systems that will eliminate routine clerical activity and provide buyers with real-time information which can be effectively used to make supply decisions. Such computer systems must truly meet the needs of the purchasing organization and not be introduced as an afterthought having provided specialized systems for manufacturing and/or accounting. Electronic data interchange (EDI) links will be established with key suppliers; however the situation will be continually monitored to ensure that these links enhance rather than inhibit purchasing performance.

SPECIFIC ISSUES

- Purchasing systems will be an integral part of the overall corporate information technology (IT) strategy. An overriding priority will be to make them easily accessible to buyer and user alike without the latter having to decide on which route procurement should be followed.

- All buying staff will have ready access to a personal computer (PC) or terminal with wordprocessing and spreadsheet capabilities and be fully trained to use them. Spreadsheet techniques will be in common use for bid compilation and evaluation.
- The requisition and purchase order routines will be computerized on a 'purpose built' user friendly system. 'Purpose built' means a system designed specifically for purchasing routines. The term does not imply bespoke; indeed it is preferred that standard commercially available packages are used. System selection will be made using one of the accepted systems analysis techniques.
- The systems should also be capable of producing data on previous purchases, spends, and commitments by supplier, cost centre, and supplier performance. The system will have links to accounts payable and the general ledger and contribute to company management information.
- EDI links will have been established with key suppliers to facilitate rapid transmissions of orders, stock levels, invoices, and payments. The use of EDI will contribute to the elimination of manually based techniques such as acknowledgement of orders and confirmation of receipts. However, great care will be taken to ensure that the use of EDI does not inhibit creative buying or suppress initiative.

Staffing and training

No purchasing operation can be effective unless it is staffed with high quality professionals who are continually updating and extending their knowledge and skills and can promote the function within their own organization.

This building block establishes the requirement for high levels of educational attainment for purchasing staff, promotes movement of high quality personnel into and out of the function, and creates high quality ongoing training programmes backed up by on-the-job coaching and counselling.

SPECIFIC ISSUES

- Purchasing staff will be well educated and professionally competent. In order to command respect company-wide, senior staff will have the same levels of educational attainment as those employed in sales, marketing, production, and finance. Ideally, staff undertaking key roles should have a degree, HNC or equivalent, together with a qualification from the relevant professional institute. Staffing with former warehouse or clerical personnel, however experienced, will not be acceptable.

- Purchasing staff will be influential, innovative, and not tied to antiquated rules. They will be change-agents, and be skilled at promoting and selling the benefits of the function.

- Staff will be a mixture of seasoned professionals and high-performing personnel on assignment (two to three years) from other functions. There will be a history of staff moving through the department on the way to more senior positions.

- There will be in place a system for running a continuous training programme for all staff—including the SPE—embracing not only core job skills but also those aimed at interpersonal skills and personal development. The training programmes should be generated by a training needs analysis of all staff. All training programmes should be the subject of programmed follow-up to ensure that the lessons learned are retained and put into practice at the workplace.
- Of special importance will be the recognition of the need to give new-comers to the function in-depth training as soon as possible.

The enabling foundation
The first steps in upgrading and changing the direction of a purchasing function come from working on these building blocks to bring them all up to the highest level. This process cannot be done overnight and it will take many months—sometimes years—to achieve the goal. However, each improvement makes it more possible to begin undertaking at least some strategic purchasing. Because of the crucial relationship of these building blocks with the entire programme, we have called them the **enabling foundation**.

The creation of this enabling foundation results in the realization of a number of important preconditions needed to implement effective strategic purchasing. These preconditions are as follows:

- clear mission for the function
- corporate commitment to the mission
- empowered buyers
- ethical behaviour
- real-time information
- high quality staff
- cross-functional teams to tackle specific issues

- a cohesive approach to the supply-market
- safe and secure contracts
- measured performance
- a reasonably stable organization
- a rational supply base.

The establishment of the enabling foundation also results in the elimination of a considerable number of unproductive and inhibiting activities. Among these are

- isolation of purchasing from corporate mainstream activity
- confused authorities
- lack of client–buyer cooperation
- fragmented approach to the market
- uncompetitive specifications
- self-generated monopolies
- too many unnecessary controls
- unsafe or insecure contracts
- non-added-value and non-productive activities
- manual routines
- poor supplier relationships.

Summary
In this chapter we have shown what organizations need to do to create an environment in which purchasing is a strategic process. When this has been achieved, the purchasing process will have the ability to make a major contribution to improvements in corporate profitability. It can play an important part in winning new business, and bringing new products to market ahead of the competition in addition to achieving significant reductions in costs.

For organizations to develop an effective purchasing strategy it requires time, patience, and a determination to make fundamental changes. It is not easy and will often be met by serious and well-entrenched objections which must be overcome by persuasive arguments couched in terms used by dynamic business people.

When the promise offered by these initiatives is delivered, in the form of strategic purchasing, the entrepreneurs responsible for the enterprise will be surprised and delighted as their businesses become increasingly profitable and have a sharper competitive edge.

3

Strategic purchasing: understanding and influencing the supply-market

Current problems

The principal strategic role of the purchasing function may be defined as seeking out and trading with suppliers of the highest quality, in terms of both the products and services offered and cost competitiveness.

Why is it then that companies with fully fledged purchasing departments frequently find themselves in disputes and difficulties with suppliers over delivery, quality, price, and other contractual terms?

It is not uncommon to find that the typical purchasing department is the scene of frantic firefighting activity with all the effort directed at solving today's immediate problems. Much of this activity is required because suppliers are failing to meet their obligations.

Why is it that suppliers so frequently fail to live up to the promises they made before the contract was awarded to them? Who is to blame? What can be done about it?

There is considerable evidence to show that these problems arise because inadequate time and resources are applied at the earliest stages of the procurement cycle. Indeed, not only are there often insufficient resources but also these have been directed towards the wrong areas.

The establishment of the enabling foundation (see Chapter 2) creates a situation in which resources can be redirected towards areas where it becomes possible to avoid many, if not all, of the above problems. The way in which this can be achieved may be understood by reference to the typical simplified version of the procurement cycle illustrated in Fig. 3.1.

The cycle starts with the identification of a need, moves through budget approval and then authority to proceed. It is usually at this stage that a requisition is raised, often the first indication that the purchasing

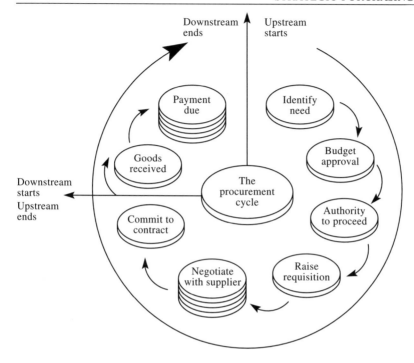

Fig. 3.1 The scale of the buyer's influence upon the supplier at different phases in the procurement cycle

department has of an impending requirement, unless purchasing has been previously involved in the negotiation.

Following the raising of the requisition, a series of supplier selection activities takes place leading up to the commitment stage, which is the placing of the order or contract.

Upstream and downstream management

We have used the term upstream management to describe all of the activities and functions which take place before the order or contract is placed; these include supply planning, the development of a contract strategy, and supplier selection.

Conversely we have called the activity which takes place after the order or contract is placed downstream management. Typically this includes expediting, inspection, problem solving, invoice matching, emergencies, and other more routine tasks, often paperwork based.

The results of examining the operations of many purchasing departments show that they spend a much higher (typically three to one) proportion of their time and resources on downstream activities than they do on upstream management. Indeed, the failure to spend sufficient skilled resources on upstream activity is the principal cause of the large downstream workload.

In this area we have developed an indicator to measure the relative performance between purchasing operations. We call this the upstream/downstream balance (UDB) which was referred to in Chapter 2. The UDB is defined as the percentage of total purchasing personnel spent on upstream activities.

The high-performing purchasing departments of the future will spend much more of their resources in upstream, where there is real potential for added-value, and in turn will find that the volume of downstream activity will shrink. As a guide we suggest that the best purchasing organizations will achieve a UDB indicator of 70 or above.

To illustrate the point let us just suppose that we have set up the right contract with the right supplier. What benefits might accrue? We might expect that:

- All deliveries will be made on time.
- There will be no need for expediting.
- There will be no quality defects.
- Paperwork from the supplier will be accurate.
- Invoices will be exact.

In other words, it will no longer be necessary for buying organizations to have to second guess their supplier. Some describe this as 'lean' purchasing.

Imagine the effect on a purchasing operation if this could be achieved. It would mean the virtual elimination of all the low-level unproductive work that currently takes place. The immediate reaction from all of those currently involved in purchasing in the real world will be 'pie in the sky'. But why should it be? Surely this should be what total quality management in the purchasing function should be aiming for.

The upstream purchasing cycle may be defined in a different way, as can be seen from Fig. 3.2. The model has been shown in this way in order to emphasize that the steps are not discrete but overlap considerably. For example, although supply planning will take place well before firm requirements are identified, the activity is likely to continue all through the identification of requirements and well into the contract strategy phase.

Figure 3.2 illustrates the five key upstream activities to which the appropriate priority and emphasis must be given. Each of these, which

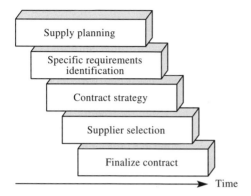

Fig. 3.2 Strategic planning phases

consist of several elements, will be dealt with in the following sections of this chapter.

Supply planning

Supply planning is an activity which should take place well before the time when it is required to take specific purchasing action. Indeed, it should not be related to a particular requisition but should be part of an ongoing programme designed to position the purchasing organization to best advantage in the marketplace.

The purpose of supply planning is

To ensure the existence of a supply-market to which the buying organization has ready access and which enables it to succeed as a business both now and in the future.

The first task is to establish the significance to the buying organization of the purchased items and then to gain an understanding of the present and possible future market conditions. This will require the use of three separate techniques:

- supply positioning
- supplier preferences
- vulnerability management.

Although these techniques will be explained in much more detail in later chapters, it is important here to give a brief overview of what they entail.

Any organization purchases a wide variety of goods and services, which will vary in value from the trivial to the multi-million pound spend. Consideration of value alone would suggest that the treatment these items receive will be related to their value. Thus low value items will receive little attention whereas major expenditures should be the subject of considerable effort. However, value alone is insufficient to determine the appropriate purchasing strategy since this will depend on both the supply-market and the criticality of the item to the buyer. **Supply positioning** (see Chapter 5) is a tool which segments purchases, both in relation to value and the degree of risk in the purchase. Clearly those items which will receive the greatest attention will be high value or high risk, especially those that are both.

The **supplier preferences** technique (see Chapter 6) looks at transactions from the point of view of the supplier. It shows how suppliers segment their customer base and how they are likely to react in a given set of circumstances. This technique then becomes even more powerful when it is combined with supply positioning in assessing the supply-market.

Vulnerability management (see Chapter 7) is a technique in which buyers examine the entire supply chain of the item that they are purchasing. By using a checklist it is possible to identify future supply problems such as shortages, interruption to supply arrangements, government restrictions, etc. Identification of issues such as these then triggers a planning activity to obviate the problem.

These three techniques are used together to define the current supply-market. They will show whether the current and predicted supply arrangements are going to be satisfactory in terms of meeting the needs of the business.

It is more than possible that some features of the current supply-market will not meet the full requirements of the buying organization either now or in the future. In relation to the marketplace, the buyers need to be deterministic in their approach. It is not enough to be knowledgeable and at the same time to accept conditions as they are. Professional buyers must determine the need and opportunity for change and develop strategies and tactics to improve those conditions to their advantage.

For example, it is insufficient to recognize that there is a cartel in operation. The deterministic buyer must devise and implement a plan to eliminate it or at least make it ineffective. In the same way buyers should be constantly seeking out alternatives when they are faced with cartels, monopolies, or general shortages.

Buyers should accordingly use a variety of additional techniques and concepts in order to change the market to their advantage.

These techniques would include

- procurement marketing
- reverse marketing
- vendor improvement—ten(d) to zero.

Again, these techniques are dealt with more fully in later chapters but a brief summary may be useful.

Procurement marketing (see Chapter 8) is the means by which buyers can market their company as a preferred customer to the supplier. Being a preferred customer brings with it a number of advantages in terms of price, service, and allocation of scarce resources in times of shortage.

Reverse marketing (see Chapter 8) is a technique to create a supply capability in the marketplace where either one does not exist or the market is set up to the disadvantage of the buyer.

Vendor improvement means what it says. Many organizations now have in place a whole series of activities designed to upgrade the performances of their suppliers. Ten(d) to zero, a play on words, is one such technique described in Chapter 8.

Vendor improvement techniques are encompassed within the framework of the affirmative vendor improvement programme and the way in which these techniques link together is shown in Fig. 3.3.

In summary the essence of strategic supply planning is that the professional buyer not only must change suppliers, but also must change the market by finding and developing new products and suppliers or by making the existing ones behave in a different way.

Special requirements identification

The second phase in the procurement cycle is the specific requirements identification. Here it must be said at once that the ultimate client user must have the final authority to decide on what is purchased. Any attempt to switch this authority to the purchasing function will be doomed to failure as responsibilities become confused and clients perceive that their legitimate rights are being usurped.

The objective of specific requirements identification may be defined as follows:

By working in a multi-functional group, to establish the true nature of the requirement and ensure that the initial interaction with suppliers and the supply-market is managed to produce the optimal result.

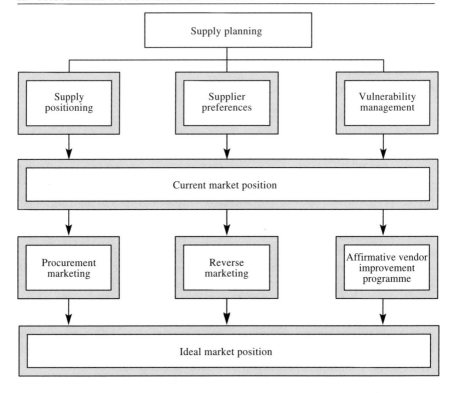

Fig. 3.3 Supply planning model

This statement clearly labels requirements identification as a multi-functional activity as opposed to one where the various functions (design, production, marketing, procurement) become involved in a sequential manner. Organizations should develop a culture where all interested parties become involved in projects at the earliest possible stage and well before any options are closed out.

The second element of the statement refers to the true nature of the requirement, therefore it is important to know what is really required as opposed to what is specified. For example, an oil company could apparently be wanting to buy road tankers, whereas what is really required is a low cost delivery system to the retail sites. Based on past experience it can be said that the identification of the true nature of the purchase has resulted in some very surprising innovations and benefits for purchasing organizations.

The third element of the statement refers to the need to manage the buyer–supplier interface at the earliest stages of a project, including understanding and exploiting the buyer–seller interest cycle. This is not to attempt to limit perfectly legitimate and necessary discussion between the technical and production staff of the two organizations but rather to ensure that in all such interchanges the staff of the buying organization are made fully aware of the implications of their actions.

What then is the role of purchasing, if any, in this phase of the cycle? Essentially the role is one of support to enable the user to take technical and financial decisions in the light of the best commercial information available. To achieve this the buyer will have to

- make the user aware of the most up-to-date supply-market information
- provide the client with accurate information regarding the cost implications of technical decisions
- suggest the use of alternative and more cost-effective products or services which could be available
- in addition to purchase price, cost effectiveness would include the costs of operation and maintenance, and of course quality and reliability where appropriate
- make the client aware of alternatives to 'outright purchase'
- provide information on the managerial and financial strengths of potential suppliers
- guide the user on how to interact with potential suppliers if it is necessary to contact them prior to the contract strategy and supplier selection phases.

This last consideration is crucial to the ultimate success or otherwise of the commercial approach. Too often, unguarded and naïve comments made by users have made it impossible for purchasing—or anyone else—to obtain the most commercially advantageous deal.

The purchasing techniques and concepts to be employed at this stage include

- market intelligence
- vendor intelligence
- interest cycling
- supplier conditioning.

The model will therefore appear as illustrated in Fig. 3.4. Interest cycling and supplier conditioning are described in Chapter 9.

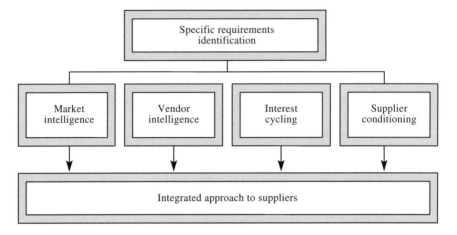

Fig. 3.4 Specific requirements identification

Contract strategy

The purpose of contract strategy is

To define the right contractual arrangements within which suppliers can make a maximum contribution to the buyer's business.

Contract strategy includes deciding on the number of sources to be used, whether contracts should be short, medium, or long term, and the intended nature of the relationship with the supply base (e.g. arm's length, cooperative, or partnership). It also takes note of prevailing market conditions and sets in place ways and means of dealing with monopolies, cartels, and other market distortions. It is concerned with the management of the risk inherent in all of these situations and the issue of supplier dependency.

The techniques which will be used in this phase are

- make vs buy analysis
- supply positioning
- supply preference analysis
- handling monopolies and cartels
- competitive advantage matrix
- supplier dependency analysis
- partnership sourcing.

This part of the model will therefore appear as shown in Fig. 3.5.

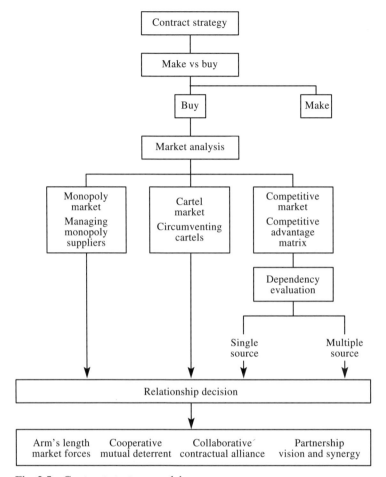

Fig. 3.5 Contract strategy model

Competitive advantage will be described in Chapter 10; partnership sourcing will be dealt with in Chapter 11; and monopolies and cartels in Chapter 12.

Supplier selection
The purpose of supplier selection is

To find the supplier that can best achieve the objectives of the contract strategy.

Supplier selection involves appraisal and evaluation, conditioning, and the methodology to be used. Methodology means deciding whether it is appropriate to tender, seek competitive quotations, take face value, or to negotiate. The techniques that will be used are

- conventional appraisal
- partnership evaluation
- buyer–supplier conditioning
- bid–negotiate matrix.

Conventional appraisal is the standard technique concerning an assessment of capability in terms of quality, delivery, and financial strength. The focus is usually on the current level of product or service which is offered, with the emphasis on the need for the supplier to offer a high level of performance or lose the business.

In a relatively limited number of cases the buying organization may wish to evaluate whether it should move towards a partnership relationship with a particular supplier. In this instance it would make use of the **partnership evaluation** technique which goes much deeper, concerning itself with assessing whether there is a true management and financial orientation fit and whether the two parties can work together for mutual benefit in the long term. This form of evaluation will include seeking evidence of

- a genuine commitment from the top to make it work
- a clear understanding by both parties concerning what is required
- the existence of capable staff trained to make the relationship work
- sufficient resources and flexibility to ensure success
- patience to overcome obstacles and teething problems
- channels of open communication between the parties
- goodwill trust implying an open commitment to resolve issues
- a culture of change and continuous improvement as the norm
- a dynamic approach to cost reduction and value enhancement.

In all relationships, of whatever type, buyers will be subjected to **conditioning** by skilled sellers. In addition to ensuring that they are fully aware of the process, buyers may wish to employ some of the techniques to reverse the process.

Finally, attention must be given to the actual method of selection. Many organizations are still obligated to use some form of competitive bidding, while others impose this obligation on themselves. Experience provides substantial evidence that while this approach is valid in many instances, it can often be quite inappropriate. Experienced buyers now make use of the **bid–negotiate matrix** to assist in deciding on the most appropriate approach.

The manner in which these techniques link together is illustrated in Fig. 3.6.

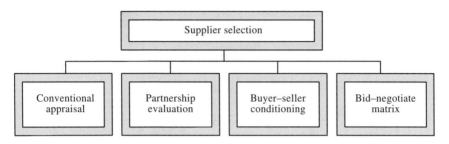

Fig. 3.6 Supplier selection techniques

Finalize contract

This is the last phase of the upstream activity and the one in which the purchasing function has traditionally played the largest part. The purpose of this phase is

> *To create a contract whose terms and conditions provide the purchasing organization with adequate protection and remedies against possible difficulties and disputes while at the same time motivating the supply organization to perform in the best possible manner.*

Included here will be understanding of all the legal, financial, and other implications associated with the placement of the contract.

Too often, and usually by default, buying organizations end up contracting on the basis of the supplier's terms. Not surprisingly these terms are always very favourable towards the supplier.

It is an important part of upstream activity to ensure that contractual terms protect and—where possible—give advantage to the buyer. The preferred position is to place all business on terms and conditions laid down by the buyer. If this is not achievable, then industry-wide standard terms should be employed.

Buyers should remember the adage that the last document passing between the parties to the contract overrides all others when deciding on the terms that apply.

Summary

The way in which all of these factors interact is illustrated in Fig. 3.7. The box at the top of the diagram sets out the goal of the purchasing function which is to contribute to corporate profit by obtaining a competitive edge, derived (in turn) from a committed and productive supply base which sees the buying organization as a preferred customer.

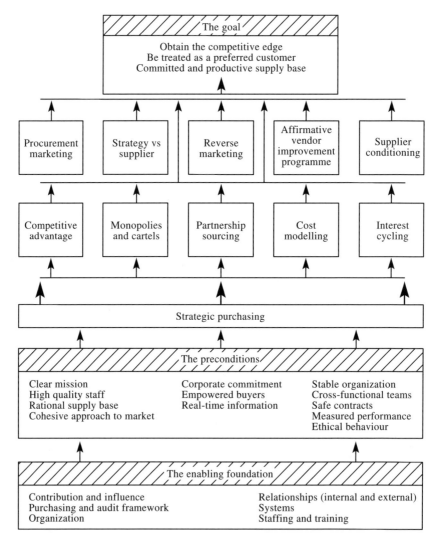

Fig. 3.7   Building for a strategic activity

The way to achieve this is by operating purchasing essentially as an 'upstream' activity. The focus of attention is on events and interactions prior to the placement of the contract or order, and not after the event (downstream activity).

Elements of upstream management include supply positioning, supplier preference, vulnerability management, procurement marketing, reverse marketing, affirmative vendor improvement programme, and partnership sourcing. Others such as monopolies and cartels, supplier conditioning, and interest cycling (see Chapter 9 and particularly Fig. 9.4 for the latter) to some extent straddle the boundary with some activity being classified as upstream, and the balance falling into downstream.

Upstream management is not possible unless the preconditions created by the enabling foundation are in place.

4

Understanding the basics of purchasing

The first three chapters of this book discussed the strategic issues surrounding the purchasing process. Before turning our attention to the detail of some of the concepts and techniques mentioned in these chapters, it is worth examining some of the basic issues which underlie the process and form the foundation for applying these new techniques.

In Chapter 1 we referred to the fact that many senior managers have little understanding of the true nature and role of the purchasing process. It is our experience that they have never seriously evaluated purchasing because they do not consider it to be of any real significance in running their business. Those who have usually make a number of false assumptions, which lead to inappropriate actions resulting in failure to make the best possible contribution to corporate profitability. This chapter examines some of these false assumptions and their possible consequences.

The first assumption challenges the need for specialist input into the purchasing process.

'Anyone can buy'

Some time ago we were asked to evaluate the purchasing activities of a major financial institution which had an annual expenditure of £800 million a year, of which £300 million was spent on information technology.

All of the expenditure on information technology (IT) was carried out and controlled by technical and operational staff as part of their normal duties. There was no purchasing function because the view was widely held that IT procurement needed to be performed by the technical specialists, since they were the only ones capable of understanding the complex requirements, and negotiating them with the suppliers.

Investigation showed that the supply organizations were consistently exploiting this situation and were failing to give the customer commercial deals which were even remotely competitive. There were problems over high prices, and requests for excessive order volumes to obtain price breaks. Several multi-million pound long-term development contracts gave all the advantages to the supplier.

How could this be allowed to happen? How was it that the company appeared quite resigned to paying more than was necessary for key supplies and prepared to become tied to contracts which were clearly disadvantageous?

The company did not deliberately set out to precipitate this state of affairs; it all happened by default. These serious shortcomings were not drawn to the attention of senior management at the right time.

It was assumed that highly trained technical personnel would be equally skilled when it came to setting and negotiating the commercial terms and conditions for the purchase orders and contracts. The reality was that the technical staff—while being expert in product knowledge—had little idea how the supply-market worked and never had any training in purchasing or in negotiation skills.

Experience gathered of many organizations and industries shows that this state of affairs is commonplace. User personnel often seem to have neither the knowledge nor the understanding and motivation to carry out commercial transactions effectively.

To take the motivational argument first, it is only necessary to examine the priorities of those specialists who are deciding on expenditure commitments for the company. For example, senior management often judges the standard of work of an engineer on whether the project is on time and works, rather than whether all the commercial terms are right and the wider financial consequences considered. The main concern is to take delivery of the equipment—perhaps at any cost—and certainly without thought for the long-term commercial implications.

The natural concern over completing the project and making it a success in technical terms often results in action in the marketplace effectively preventing the company achieving the most effective deal. It is common practice for users to tell potential suppliers—with an ensuing loss of negotiating leverage—the amount in the budget, that they have been selected, or that there is no real competition. Not unexpectedly, these actions result in budgets frequently being exceeded.

Even if the motivation is present, the untrained purchaser will make a number of assumptions, which can be completely erroneous, about the market forces (discussed later in this chapter). Unfortunately, many full-time purchasing personnel also share these false assumptions and so are ill equipped to explain to senior management the key reasons as to why commercial transactions entailing significant expenditure should be influenced by trained professional purchasers.

'Price is always related to cost'

There is a widespread view that prices asked by suppliers are always closely related to the cost of production. In other words, the supplier calculates the price by totalling the costs and then adding on a margin for profit.

Nothing could be further from the truth. A supplier may set prices in this way, but is more likely to be pursuing pricing strategies which take a large number of other factors into consideration. Close attention would be paid to the state of the market, the supplier's own financial position, the stage in the product life cycle, and the supplier's own long-term goals.

These price strategies may result in high, average, or low prices. For example, a supplier trying to enter a market, increase market share, make stock reductions, or keep out a competitor may decide to drop prices—even below cost—in the short term, in order to achieve one of these objectives. Conversely, a supplier trying to exploit a monopoly position or product scarcity may raise prices to very high levels.

Pricing policies may vary throughout the life cycle of a product to meet specific sales and revenue objectives. Examples abound where price can be used to expand and extend a market, keep out competition, maximize on a technical advantage, and sustain revenue at a time of declining sales.

'Price is always related to volume'

'I have no chance of getting highly competitive prices because I only buy small quantities'. This is one of the most common statements heard when talking to buyers from many organizations. There is no better illustration of the seller's powers of suggestion and this is what sellers would have all buyers believe; it serves their undisclosed purpose—which is to sell higher volumes—and to resist price challenges.

One of the most effective tools used by suppliers is the price list. Lists always have one common characteristic; the more you buy, the lower the unit price. A further refinement is the price break mechanism, where special discounts are offered in return for achieving certain volume.

The argument which attempts to legitimize this stance advances the hypothesis that costs of production and supply reduce, as purchase volumes increase. There may be justification for this, such as the cost of partial-vs-full loads, reduced sales effort, and machinery set-up times. However, purchasers should be wary of accepting this argument at face value and be prepared to question in detail. There is considerable evidence to suggest that on certain occasions, and in some situations, small volume buyers can achieve lower unit prices than buyers of much higher volumes. Examples can be found in the buying of sugar, fuels, cement, advertising, engines, and computers, to name but a few.

The overriding message is

Small volume buyers need to start with a view that lower unit prices are attainable. If they work hard to achieve them, the results can be dramatic.

'Buyer power increases with the size of the organization'
Buyers for large organizations have often been heard to say

Suppliers will always offer us the best deal because we are a well-known 'blue chip' company.

The implication is that all suppliers will fall over themselves to supply a company because it has a high standing in the business world. Whereas this is commonplace it is not always the position. One of the biggest problems facing large organizations is becoming over-confident about their position; they fail to see that their attitude—and perhaps some of their terms of business—make them less attractive to certain suppliers. Sometimes they are consequently offered less favourable terms than their competitors.

The situation frequently arises where a buyer from such an organization takes a large percentage of a supplier's output, and confidently assumes that their deal is more favourable on that account. However, it is most likely that the suppliers' quoted prices will include—at a minimum—a *full* share of the overhead costs, as apportioned to that job, whereas the buyer of a smaller quantity sometimes obtains supplies that are costed on a marginal basis.

Professional buyers need to be continually aware of this danger and should take positive steps to ensure that the appropriate image is transmitted to the marketplace.

'Price lists are set in stone'

Price lists are used to encourage the buyer to increase purchase quantities. They also serve another purpose: to make the asking price look legitimate—and not negotiable.

A very well printed and presented price list, perhaps together with a discount structure and order form, has a permanent look about it. Many buyers appear to be intimidated by such documents and become reluctant to challenge the basic pricing structures which they contain. This is, of course, precisely what the price list documentation is intended to do.

Professional buyers should be prepared to challenge the very basis of such documents. Tearing up a price list in front of a seller is an extreme but sometimes effective way of getting the message across.

'Competitive bidding gets the best prices'

It is still true that many purchasing organizations believe that competitive bidding will usually result in the most beneficial deals and—more to the point—the lowest prices. It is common practice to have rules which require the use of the competitive bidding process for all purchases above a certain value, itself set at a lower point. It is of major concern that this practice has now become the foundation of the European Union (EU) Directives on Public Procurement.

It is remarkable that this view is still held despite the mounting evidence which suggests the contrary. Certain professional purchasers have always questioned this view but the subject was not given wide debate until the 1984 Report to the Prime Minister on Government Purchasing.[1]

Section 3.33 of this report says

> *Further evidence that the competitive tendering is no guarantee of best value for money comes from our discussions with the private sector. Nearly all the companies visited saw receiving the bids in response to a competitive tender, not as the end of the purchasing process, but as one stage in it ... there is evidence in the way in which foreign countries approach government purchasing which argues that a planned approach provides better value for money.*

The report then goes on to report examples to support the contention.

Our investigations fully support this view but we have gone on to try to determine why this should be so. Theoretically, if suppliers know that they are competing with each other, and truly want the business, then surely they are going to submit their best offer the first time.

We have concluded that the following factors militate against always getting the best price:

- It could be that some bidders really do not want the business because of capacity restraints or other factors. These bidders will put in high 'cover' prices to avoid causing offence or appearing to be unwilling to bid and to ensure that they are asked next time. This could well leave only unproductive or inefficient suppliers truly bidding competitively.
- Bidders may not be convinced that the business is *really* on offer. Buyers frequently go out to bid merely to get information on which to base negotiations with incumbent suppliers whom they do not want to change. Suppliers understand this and will not spend time on preparing a sharply competitive bid which will not be considered.
- The preparation of a really competitive bid takes considerable time and effort. Suppliers receive many enquiries and cannot be sure of those where they have a real chance of success. As a result they often use a costing estimating system which will result in a fair bid but not the best possible one. It is not worth the effort to fine-tune in many cases.
- Many of the intangible, but nevertheless potentially valuable factors in an offer, may not emerge as part of a written bid process. For example, the supplier may well have expertise which could reduce costs, or improve the product at the design stage. It is only when the two parties start to discuss a business opportunity that innovative—and possibly highly productive ideas—may be produced.

For these reasons buying organizations will receive the most competitive offers possible only if they behave in such a way as to make the potential supplier ready to work really hard to win the business. Whereas this may be achieved by competitive bidding, other techniques may often realize better results.

Professional buyers should take these factors into account in preparing their acquisition plans and their company purchasing policies should be designed to give them freedom to make appropriate commercial decisions.

'Negotiation downwards endangers service and quality'

This is another stock comment from users when first confronted with the suggestion that purchasing is going to be done in a different way, possibly by making more use of negotiation.

This comment is again based on the belief that suppliers will have already submitted the lowest price and that to move them below that implies that they will have to recover their income in another way. The assumption is that there must be a loss in service or quality. 'You get what you pay for' is the cry.

As noted above, sellers do not always submit their best prices first time and some margin for further improvement often exists. Furthermore, we have not been able to find any conclusive evidence to support the loss of service and quality claimed in the short term. However, it should be pointed out that where there is a long-term emphasis on price and price reduction within a market—as is the case with the UK construction industry, for example—there is a risk of accompanying poor performance.

'Sealed bidding is the most secure method'

Most organizations rely to some extent on the sealed bidding process in order to purchase their requirements. There are wide differences in the minimum values at which the process starts, from as low as £500 to as high as £500 000.

Organizations which use this method share the view that sealed bidding is, in some way, a more secure purchasing process, much less exposed to dishonest behaviour than other acquisition strategies. In fact, there are many ways in which the process can be distorted to achieve unethical objectives, such as rigging the bid list and providing the suppliers with differing amounts of information.

In some companies there have been instances of fraudulent behaviour using a sealed bid process, arising, in part, because management and auditors alike placed undue faith in the integrity of the process and ceased to be alert to these possibilities. Purchasing management should look again at their sealed bidding policies and procedures to ensure that they are used effectively and only in situations which merit them.

'Multiple sourcing increases competition'

In developing sourcing policies, companies frequently instigate rules which require buyers to ensure that all key supplies have at least two sources. The reasons given for this are to ensure security of supply and to maintain competition.

The argument for security of supply stems from the concerns about what would happen if a sole supplier experienced difficulties due to plant failures, strikes, transportation, interruptions, or lack of raw-materials. The existence of a second, and alternative supplier, would enable the buying organization to switch demand with minimal disruption. There is no doubt that this argument has some validity for critical supplies but it is certainly questionable whether its application in all cases delivers the benefits claimed.

The second reason which relates to maintaining competition is less valid. This is certainly so if the buying organization consistently goes out to competitive bidding and then splits the business, say 60–40, in favour of the lowest two bidders. Indeed, some companies adopt this policy even when there are only two bidders; each bidder is already sure of 40 per cent and it is therefore questionable how competitive they will be to gain the extra 20 per cent.

Maintaining several sources for a particular commodity or service can have a profound impact on the way the suppliers see the business. Figure 4.1 illustrates the impact that long-term contracting strategies can have on supplier responses in the single and multiple sourcing situations.

	Single sourcing	Multiple sourcing
Short-term contracting (0 to 1 years)	Future uncertain Need staffing flexibility Minimal investment Deteriorated learning High selling costs Limited quality improvement Low commitment Innovation unlikely	Future uncertain Volume uncertain Need staffing flexibility Will have peaks and troughs Minimal investment Deteriorated learning High selling costs Limited quality improvement Very low commitment Innovation zero
Medium-term contracting (1 to 3 years)	Short time horizons Reluctance to take on staff Short payout investment Limited efficiency programmes Improved learning curve Moderate commitment Some innovation	Short time horizons Need staff flexibility Minimal investment No efficiency programmes Moderate learning curve Limited commitment Innovation unlikely
Long-term contracting (4 + years)	Future predictable Optimal staffing and training High capital investment Product development Good efficiency programmes Steep learning curve Minimal paperwork High commitment Complacency (potential danger) Commitment to innovate Partnership probable	Volumes uncertain Smaller volumes Staffing uncertain Moderate capital investment Efficiency programmes Steep learning curve Maintains competitive edge Moderate commitment Innovation unlikely

Fig 4.1 Impact of purchasing strategies on supplier response

Short-term contracting and multiple sourcing create uncertainty about both the volume of business and future orders. Incentives for the supplier to invest in quality and other improvements are low and the supplier's commitment to the buyer will not be high.

With longer-term multiple sourcing contracts there will be moderate investment in efficiencies and quality improvements but this will still be inhibited by uncertainty as to volume.

Moving to single sourcing will improve attitudes in both long- and short-term contracts. With long-term single sourcing, the supplier has the confidence to invest capital in efficiency programmes and product development. It also allows the supplier to stabilize staffing levels and minimize paperwork. There should be a high level of commitment but it should be remembered that these same conditions can breed complacency.

In summary, the move to multiple sourcing may have the opposite of the desired effect, especially if operated in conjunction with short-term contracting.

'Partnerships benefit the buyer'

There is a wide body of opinion in the purchasing profession which now favours the development of buyer–supplier partnerships as the pre-ferred—and most effective way—of doing business. The rationale is that a long-term relationship with a single source provides opportunities for mutual development and improvement, thus benefiting both parties.

The concept is based on the widely publicized experiences of Japanese manufacturers within their own country. While the techniques do have application elsewhere it is important to be aware that their success is in part due to the special nature of the Japanese industrial culture (mutual shareholdings and long-term links between businesses, among other features). This culture does not exist as widely in Europe thus making the transplant more difficult. This is not to say that the partnership concept has no application outside the Japanese sphere of business but rather to point out that its introduction will require very careful thought and planning. A prerequisite of such relationships is an open culture and effective communication channels. Experience shows that where partner-ships fail, leading to the selection of an unproductive supplier, it is often because of the buyer's lack of openness, unwillingness to think long term, or an inadequate view of the market at the outset. This topic is discussed in more detail in Chapter 11.

'Price formulae protect the buyer'

When entering into long-term contracts it is not always possible to be specific about price for the entire duration. In this situation buyers often resort to the use of formulae to calculate future process. Such a formula could be the general Retail Price Index, an industry specific—such as BEAMA (British Electrotechnical and Allied Manufacturers' Associations) or NEDO (National Economic Development Office)—or a formula specially designed for the particular contract.

Certainly these formulae are of value but buyers should beware of using them without frequent comparison to the actual prices in the supply-market. Without constant vigilance it is possible for these formula-based prices to be very much above the competitive rates. For example, in a recent study[2] for a printing works we found that a long-established formula had resulted in the buyer paying a price for paper which was twice as high as could be obtained with competitive suppliers.

Be assured that suppliers will often rapidly bring to the attention of the buyer any adverse movements to their own position and hence request changes to a formula. They are less likely to bring to the buyer's attention the reverse situation.

'The buyer has no power when dealing with a monopoly'

Again this is a commonly held view with the inevitable result that many buyers give up and accept what is asked. However, the situation is by no means this clear-cut.

First, many apparent monopolies are nothing of the kind. Either they have been created by a poor specification or the sourcing is insufficient or not broadly based enough. A change of specification or more comprehensive sourcing could dramatically improve this situation.

Even when there is a true monopoly all is not lost and there are many actions that the buyer can take to alleviate the problem. These actions are described in Chapter 12.

'Payments do not matter'

In the course of performing appraisals of purchasing operations across the industrial spectrum it has become apparent that many companies are regarded by their suppliers as poor payers. Payments are often very late and made only after persistent reminders.

Further investigation has revealed that, in many instances, late payment is the result of deliberate decisions in support of other objectives of financial management. Finance departments—without any reference to purchasing departments—take decisions to delay payments for several weeks. This is regarded as a good cost-saving initiative.

In fact, in the long term, the reverse will almost certainly be the case. At best, if companies get a poor reputation, then suppliers will inflate prices to compensate. At worst, certain of the most productive and efficient suppliers may decline to trade. The impact of such reactions on corporate profitability can be very substantial indeed.

Summary

Understandably, the comments made in this chapter will not apply in every situation in which buyers find themselves; in fact there will quite often be occasions where one or more of these assumptions will be operating in combination, the point being that buyers should not act on the basis that these assumptions are always true but should strive to ensure that they are tested as frequently as possible.

Professionally trained staff should take time to explain some of these concepts to management and technical staff. Creating an understanding about the real nature of the marketplace—and the opportunities it presents—will assist purchasers to demonstrate the unique and specialist skills which they can contribute to the business.

Notes and references

1. HMSO (1984) *Government Purchasing: Review of Government Contracting and Procurement Procedures. A Report to the Prime Minister.*
2 Private study. Unpublished.

5

Supply positioning

Chapter 1 referred to the difficulties of implementing strategic purchasing because many senior managers see the process as essentially a tactical activity concerned only with day-to-day routines. In the minds of many, the purchasing department is there to take care of the routine tasks and to lean on suppliers should delivery be late.

Many senior managers draw a distinction between these routine items and the really important purchases including capital. It is therefore not unusual to find that the purchasing department is buying the trivia whereas the significant items are being bought by managers outside of the function, particularly in technical and engineering areas. As we have seen in the previous chapters, this often results in poor and uncompetitive terms for the buying organization.

In the past, purchasing professionals seeking to gain a wider involvement have done themselves a disservice by focusing on negotiation and price management as the main areas for their potential contribution—they have also treated all purchases in the same way—whereas, in reality, the total purchasing requirement of an organization has widely disparate characteristics requiring different priorities and objectives. The buyers' myopic preoccupations have largely contributed to their rejection by other functions as being capable of adding value because 'purchasing is concerned only with price'.

Even when purchasing departments are assigned full responsibility for all purchases, it is not unusual to find that buyers are using inappropriate approaches to the marketplace and to specific suppliers and they can struggle with the establishment of objectives and priorities.

The supply positioning technique[1] provides a mechanism for discriminating between the components of the total purchasing requirement, whether goods or services, and a tool for developing specific strategies to meet the needs of the organization with respect to each group of purchases. It can also be a very powerful means of convincing senior management of the really effective role that purchasing can play in contributing to corporate success.

Before considering supply positioning, it is necessary to review Pareto analysis.

Pareto analysis

In attempting to differentiate between purchases, most textbooks make reference to Pareto analysis. This will now be described so that the reader can obtain a complete overview of the options available.

If a graph is made of the total value of all the purchases which an organization makes against the number of items purchased, starting with the highest value item, then for nearly all cases the curve shown in Fig. 5.1 is obtained.

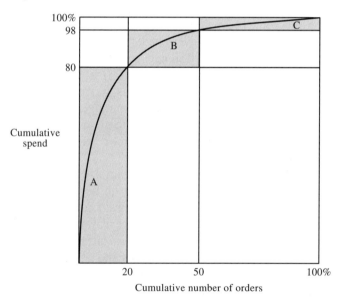

Fig. 5.1 Purchasing and the Pareto curve: the concept

This curve has two important characteristics. The best known is the 80/20 rule, where 80 per cent of all the items account for 20 per cent of the total value and conversely the 20 per cent highest value items account for 80 per cent of the spend. The second characteristic is less well known and is that 50 per cent of the range can often account for less than 2 per cent of the total spend.

The shape of the curve will vary from organization to organization.

IMPLICATIONS FOR A BUYING ORGANIZATION

Pareto analysis has two main implications for a buying organization:

• From the point of view of direct financial impact on the business, little effort need be spent on placing the lowest 50 per cent of all orders. Good, or poor, buying will have no significant impact on profitability and cost.
• Concentration on the 20 per cent highest value orders will have the greatest impact on profit and cost. This therefore is where the most effort should be placed.

It is interesting to note (as discussed previously) that these top 20 per cent of orders for 'important items' are often entrusted to areas outside of the purchasing department whereas the lowest 50 per cent, by value, are almost entirely the responsibility of the department.

LIMITATIONS OF PARETO ANALYSIS

While Pareto analysis does provide some guidance to the setting of priorities, it fails to take account of the many other considerations which surround the purchasing decision. Thus this guidance relates only to the direct financial levels and does not consider the relative importance of items bought, or extend to developing tactics and strategies to approach the market and individual suppliers.

Pareto analysis has two main limitations for a buying organization:

• Pareto analysis fails to identify those low value items which, if they fail, or are not available, could have a disproportionate effect on the operability and hence profitability of the buying organization. For example, a pipe connector is of low value but, if it fails in service, a large section of pipeline might have to be dug up in order to find and replace it. Similarly, the non-availability of a low cost bearing or seal could shut down a production line.
• Pareto analysis fails to discriminate between the methods which should be used to obtain high value goods and services when these will be highly dependent upon such factors as product availability, numbers of suppliers, and criticality to the operation. Obviously the approach to purchasing a high value item which is in plentiful supply and has no special technical considerations will be quite different from that used

when the buyer is faced with monopoly supplier for an item with a very high quality specification.

The recognition of these limitations led to the development of **supply positioning**. This tool is now being applied widely in the making of purchasing decisions.

Setting up a supply positioning analysis

The first step in developing a supply positioning analysis is to list all the goods and services which are purchased for the organization *regardless* of who actually does the buying. In itself this can be a time-consuming process but it is essential that all commitments—of whatever type—are included.

The second step is to plot each of these items on a two-dimensional chart in which the X axis represents the relative cost of the item (or category) and the Y axis represents supply exposure or potential vulnerability (see Fig. 5.2).

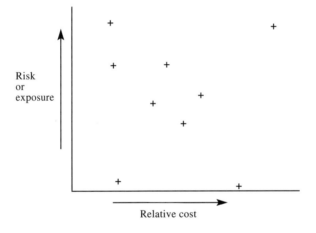

Fig. 5.2 Setting up supply positioning analysis

The relative cost parameter represents the importance of the item or category in terms of its annual cost compared to the total expenditure of the organization. Cost here is the total annual expenditure rather than the unit price; hence a million items at £1 each totalling £1 million annually would represent a significant item in these terms.

A category which accounts for more than say 0.5 per cent of total expenditure on goods and services would be located towards the middle of the X axis and would move further to the right as this proportion increases. Conversely low value items would be positioned towards the left hand end of the *X* axis.

Each organization will have to define the *Y* axis according to its own situation and needs. For most it will be a mixture of the following:

1 *Supply availability*   If the item is in plentiful supply and there are a large number of suppliers, then it will be placed low on the *Y* axis. Shortages or a limitation on the number of suppliers will position it higher on this axis.
2 *Quality requirements*   If specifications are such that very high qualities or tight tolerances are required then the item will be positioned high on the *Y* axis. Common industrial standards or lack of quality requirements will tend to place it in a lower position.
3 *Safety/environmental reliability*   If there are overriding and important safety/environmental reliability considerations, the item will be high on the *Y* axis. Absence of these will position the item lower down.

This initial positioning will be the subject of vigorous discussion as individual managers may well hold different views as to the relative importance and exposure of some items. This can be very beneficial in arriving at the agreed positioning and is why it is recommended that the exercise be a joint activity shared by all of the managers within and preferably outside of the purchasing function as well.

Supply-market segmentation
With the initial positioning complete, the next stage is to segment the market by dividing the chart into four quadrants as shown in Fig. 5.3.

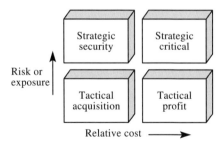

Fig. 5.3   The supply positioning analysis

Each of the four quadrants has been assigned a name which in part describes the nature of the items within it.

Thus the items in the bottom left quadrant will be of low value and have a low exposure because they have no special quality, safety, reliability, or environmental (Q/S/R/E) implications and there are many suppliers in the market able to meet buyer demand. These items are classified as **tactical acquisition**.

The items in the top left quadrant are also of low value but in this case there are either quality, safety, reliability, or environmental considerations and/or there is a shortage of product or suppliers. Included in this category, which is called **strategic security**, might be goods obtained from a monopoly supplier or items with very tight tolerances and specifications. These items are critical to the operation but are low in relative cost terms.

The bottom right quadrant contains items which are of relatively high cost but where there are no quality, safety, reliability, or environmental problems and where there are plenty of suppliers. These items are classified as **tactical profit**.

Finally the items in the top right quadrant are classified as **strategic critical** because they are of high cost and either have a significant quality, safety, reliability, or environmental factors or are drawn from a difficult market in which there are few supplies and suppliers. As the name implies, these are critical to the overall profitability, competitiveness, and success of the buying organization.

Purchasing goals
It will be seen that the items in the four quadrants have considerably diverse characteristics. Not surprisingly the purchasing goals and objectives will be quite different in each of them. Fig. 5.4 demonstrates this.

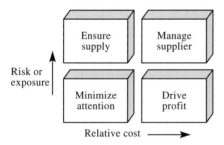

Fig. 5.4 Supply positioning and purchasing goals

There will be a myriad of items which fall into the category of **tactical acquisition** and they will form a large proportion of the 50 per cent lowest value orders of the Pareto analysis. These items, being of low value and having low exposure, are those on which the minimum amount of time and resource should be spent. The objective will be to automate and/or delegate the purchasing processes as far as is possible and to **minimize the attention** which they are given.

Many senior managers when faced with this proposition will insist that all purchases should be made using traditional and time-consuming methods. The response must be to point out that resources are always finite and that therefore it is necessary to be selective. A 20 per cent improvement in the price of the tactical acquisition items will result in a saving of 0.4 per cent of total spend, whereas a 5 per cent improvement on the high value items will result in tenfold savings of 4 per cent. It should also be noted that price is but one of the benefits that can accrue from the targeting of good purchasing practices to the high value end of the portfolio.

Strategic security items, while being of low value, are nevertheless critical to the success of the business. Here the major goal will be to **ensure supplies**, albeit even, if necessary, at some price premium, since overall the business has to be insensitive to the cost of these items. Nevertheless, these items should be kept under frequent review to ensure that they do not become a major cost item (and thus move to the right) and efforts should be made to find ways of being able to categorize them as tactical acquisition. Buyers will keep close to the supply-market, watching out for movements in the supplier base and technical innovations.

Tactical profit items are of relatively high cost but have no major complications with respect to quality, safety, and reliability. In addition, there will be an adequate number of competitive suppliers. It is in this area that buyers can seek out opportunities to cut cost and **drive for profit** using innovation and competition. With an easy supply-market they can afford to take risks and 'wheel and deal'. Buyers will need to be very knowledgeable of the supply-market within which they are operating.

The situation in the last category, **strategic critical**, is quite different. These items are of high cost and so every effort has to be made to reduce their financial impact but at the same time it is not possible to trade in the manner suggested for tactical profit. It will be essential to ensure availability of supply but close price management will also be necessary. All items must be kept under continuous review, hopefully with the objective of finding new suppliers or overcoming some of the special considerations which prevent the use of competition. Buyers will keep in very close touch with the supply-market, monitoring supply–demand balances, and vendor dependencies; much effort will be spent in **managing existing suppliers** to ensure that they are capable of meeting current—and future—demands.

Purchasing action scenarios

The foregoing has concentrated on the differing goals and objectives within the four quadrants. To develop the concept further, appropriate purchasing actions which might be taken in support of these goals are now examined. These are illustrated in Figs 5.5, 5.6, 5.7 and 5.8.

Further analysis of the supply positioning action scenarios follows in the rest of this chapter, taking the quadrants in the same order as before.

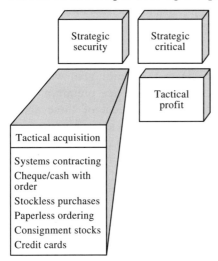

Fig. 5.5   Tactical acquisition action scenarios

TACTICAL ACQUISITION (TA)
See Fig. 5.5. The main objective is, as far as is possible, to 'minimize attention' of the entire purchasing process while ensuring probity, and to commit as few resources to it as are necessary. This can be achieved in a number of ways:

● Allowing user groups to make direct one-off purchases without the need to refer to the purchasing department. Instead of completing a requisition to be passed to purchasing for action, the user completes a simplified purchase order. Purchasing involvement is limited to creating and implementing a simplified purchase order process which is easy to use, but at the same time provides a record of the transactions for subsequent control and analysis.

- Creating term purchase agreements or blanket orders which enable users to place repeat orders directly on selected suppliers but where all terms and conditions have been previously agreed.

- Setting up service agreements to reduce the amount of in-house activity required in the process. As an example, for many organizations the purchase of stationery would fall into the TA category. Following this principle many companies have for example eliminated their own stationery stores and set up service contracts with specialist stationery suppliers who can provide a fast and responsive service, as well as delivering directly to the point of use. Under the terms of these contracts the users (often support staff) place regular (twice a week) requests directly with the stationers for next-day delivery straight to their own desks. Although in some cases a small premium may sometimes be paid, considerable savings are made by eliminating stockholding and resources are released to handle more important items.

- Grouping together a number of small items into a larger package and establishing one supplier to handle all of them. For example, one factory has grouped together office cleaning, gardening, pest control, and janitorial supplies into one service contract. Another example is the employment of a forms management contractor to minimize the effort on forms design and acquisition; this has eliminated the need to place a large number of print orders on a regular basis. Not only do these arrangements result in reduced effort but also lower costs have been achieved with the supplies due to the contractors' purchasing power.

- Streamlining payment systems and eliminating the need for invoices. Systems would include cheque with order, providing users with company cheque books or charge cards and supplier direct debit or self-payment using a buyer company cheque. Providing suitable control mechanisms are put in place, all of these can be satisfactorily accomplished without undue risk or exposure.

Overall, the emphasis in the tactical acquisition quadrant should be to take action which will assist in the clarity of the objective of the core activity, by minimizing effort to ensure that management focus is placed on those areas which can really deliver a difference to corporate performance.

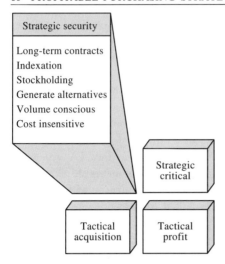

Fig. 5.6   Strategic security action scenarios

As a result of implementing these purchasing scenarios we would expect to see a decrease in stockholding, cost control, measurement, personnel, and paperwork. We would expect to see a marginal increase in price vulnerability but this would be offset by increased user accountability and budgetary control.

Purchasing would be local or, at the most, national. In line with the theme of minimizing attention would be the mental set of 'organize and let it go'.

STRATEGIC SECURITY (SS)
See Fig. 5.6. In the strategic security category the emphasis is on long-term contracts with the use of indices and formulae to fix price and the setting up of buffer stocks to achieve security of supply. Both indexation and buffer stocks are reasonable propositions in this scenario where the annual cost of items is relatively low and thus the search for competitive value for money is not paramount.

In many, but not all organizations, spares fit into this category. Although the cost of a given spare may be very low its failure or lack of availability could result in a costly shutdown of the plant or factory. Thus it may be important to maintain very high quality standards while at the same time ensuring that the buying organization keeps buffer stocks or agrees with suppliers that they will do so.

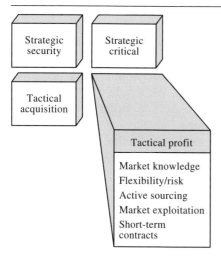

Fig. 5.7   Tactical profit action scenarios

Overall the emphasis in this strategic security area is to assist the flexibility of the buying organization. We would expect to see a decrease in the sensitivity to price, vulnerability/risk, number of orders and payments. There is likely to be an increase in stock and price and an opportunity to make more use of electronic data interchange (EDI).

It may be necessary to source on a regional, or even global basis. In line with the theme of security of supply would be a mental set of 'reduce the problem'.

TACTICAL PROFIT (TP)
See Fig. 5.7. The priority within the tactical profit category would be on short-term contracts to enable the buyer to deliver lower cost from a flexible supply-market by changing supplier as necessary. Buyers would pursue a very active sourcing policy to find new suppliers or new services and products. They will be driven by the need to make a significant contribution to corporate profit by reducing costs in this premium area.

In the hotel industry it is possible that carpeting would be treated in this way. There are a great number of suppliers and the quality is now defined by national standards so the seeking out of more competitive deals can be undertaken without taking unacceptable risks. Nevertheless, the buyer operating in this field would require a detailed knowledge of the market and would have to be an able negotiator.

Overall the emphasis on tactical profit will be to generate margin; that is, to use competitive purchase prices to increase corporate profitability.

As a result we would expect to see a decrease in unit price, security, and detailed knowledge of specific suppliers. We would expect to see an increase in market knowledge, the number of orders, timing and sensitivity of order placement, and change.

Sourcing will range from local to international. In line with a theme of 'wheeling and dealing' to maximize profit, the mental set is that of 'trade'.

STRATEGIC CRITICAL (SC)

See Fig. 5.8. The strategic critical category will require the highest level of buying skills. In some circumstances, long-term contracts may be very suitable but in others, medium-term contract lengths would be preferred. Buyers will need to obtain detailed information on individual suppliers and be seeking to develop with them to mutual advantage. It is in this area where the 'partnership' concept may most effectively be used. Price must be closely monitored and controlled by monitoring and managing price variance. All of the items will need to be kept under continuous review to ensure that suppliers can continue to supply and that prices are kept within agreed parameters.

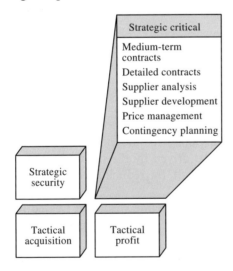

Fig. 5.8 Strategic critical action scenarios

An example of this category would be a relatively high value chemical constituent in the production of a drug in which the number of suppliers may be limited and the material itself may be in short supply. Buyers must work closely with the suppliers in order to seek innovative methods of ensuring production delivery and cost targets are met. Additionally, there is a need to ensure that product innovation and development are continuous in this key area.

Overall the emphasis in this strategic critical area will be to assist competitiveness. This is wider than just price advantage and would include rapid innovation, earlier time to market and superior product quality.

As a result we would expect to see a decrease in both the number of orders and the use of competitive bidding. There may well be an increase in buying consortia, currency risk, purchase price and cost analysis, supplier knowledge, and eventually, partnerships.

Sourcing could be international, national, or regional, and in line with the theme of managing the supplier, the mental set is likely to be 'checking/searching': checking where we are, searching to do better.

Other applications

So far this chapter has discussed the application of supply positioning to the approach to the supply-market and suppliers. It can also be used to provide a framework for managing other aspects of activity within the purchasing organization.

Some of these other applications, which include staffing and training and measurement, will be discussed in later chapters. One application for discussion now is its use in deciding on action within conglomerates or organizations with many operating locations.

Conglomerates' purchasing

Conglomerates are characterized by a large number of mostly self-sufficient companies or units each responsible for their own profit and loss. Each may have its own purchasing function but in certain cases there will be a group purchasing directorate, sometimes with unclear authorities and responsibilities.

Experience has shown that there is often tension, if not outright hostility, between the company purchasing units and the group directorate. On the one hand clear guidance may not be given on when to cooperate and in which areas, on the other hand the focus on individual company profit within a group may wreck corporate purchasing initiatives.

Supply positioning can be used in order to make this clear. The four quadrants are reproduced in Fig. 5.9 but this time with descriptions of corporate and separate actions included.

TACTICAL ACQUISITION

In the area of tactical acquisition it will be noted that there are two principal courses of action, namely, the setting up of corporate blanket orders, and concentration on the use of local suppliers. Clearly with the emphasis on service and placement of orders by the clients it follows local suppliers with a local presence would be preferred in the majority of cases since they will be able to provide a more responsive service than those situated a distance away.

The exception would be corporate blanket orders, which in this case, would be put into place to provide a series of contracts which can be utilized with the minimum of effort, in order to purchase items under previously agreed terms and conditions, and to provide a high quality service. In this area price has a relatively low priority.

For example, in many companies this approach would apply to short-term car-hire. The establishment of a national or international contract for car-hire would enable any authorized person in any of the group companies to buy the service with the minimum of effort. Terms and conditions (including a reasonable discount) will have been previously

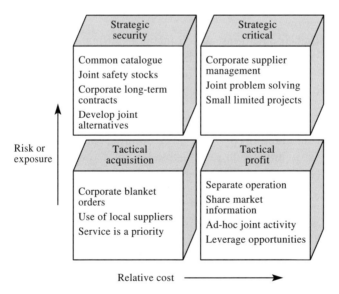

Fig. 5.9 Supply positioning analysis applied to conglomerates

agreed and the overall service level specified. The fact that it might be possible to obtain the service at a lower cost, due to local conditions or specific promotions, would be irrelevant since the organization would not wish its staff to spend time trying to optimize this type of purchase. The time and effort to do so cannot be justified and the individual will be better utilized if focused on areas with higher added-value potential.

STRATEGIC SECURITY

In the strategic security area the corporation may benefit from having a common catalogue so that companies can establish joint safety stocks and assist each other with urgent requirements. It will also be beneficial to set up long-term corporate contracts for the supply of certain key items. The drive here will be to remove the risk by establishing the buyer as a significant customer worthy of preference and priority handling (e.g. consignment stocking).

TACTICAL PROFIT

In the tactical profit area it is most likely that the companies will wish to undertake separate activities, given the difficulties in making the decision to change suppliers quickly on a corporate basis. Here the concept of corporate blanket orders always runs into trouble because of the time taken to collect the relevant data and the fact that it is almost impossible to offer all participants a deal which is better (or in some cases as good) as the one that they have established locally. A key activity is to share market information, thus providing buyers with a wealth of data on which to develop their own deals. Further work can be done on an ad-hoc basis on solving specific problems or exploiting opportunities.

STRATEGIC CRITICAL

In the strategic critical area it may be decided that it is important to manage selected key suppliers on a group basis. It is likely that such close supplier management would be undertaken by the group pur-chasing directorate unless the organization had set up a sophisticated system under which the supplier could be managed by a lead affiliate. It may be possible to set up corporate deals in order to maximize leverage but an essential prerequisite would be to find ways of streamlining the process of data gathering, information analysis, and decision making. Whichever route is followed it is essential that all parties who wish to participate in the arrangement are involved in its overall strategy and subsequently support it.

Summary

The supply positioning technique lends itself to universal purchasing utilization, however large or small the company or the department, and whatever the end product or service. The extent of application can depend on the expenditure value, the criticality of the materials, the systems in place, and the resources available. Potentially, the exploitation of supply positioning can lift the purchasing activity out of the tactical, firefighting, rut, into a strategic role within the organization, contributing significantly to profit, cashflow, and corporate development.

Notes and references

1 Elliott Shircore, T. I. and Steele, P. T. (1985) 'Procurement positioning overview', *Purchasing and Supply Management, Official Journal of the Institute of Purchasing and Supply*, December.

6

Supplier preferences

Many companies are now using supply positioning to analyse their supply-market and develop purchasing strategies related to the various resulting quadrants. However, in this model no consideration has been given to the approach and attitude of the individual supplier, the effect that this will have on relationships and consequently the success or otherwise of the commercial interchange.

It does not, for example, make any predictions or provide guidance concerning the willingness or reluctance of the supplier to service the customer in the manner desired by the latter. Full account needs to be taken of the supplier's views of the supply positioning for the technique to be effectively applied—with the consequent realization of the potential benefits.

Key account management
In trying to define such supplier attitudes it may be helpful to review certain changes which have been taking place within the more sophisticated sales organizations since the mid-1980s. Many such organizations have moved away from the traditional promotion of volume sales, regardless of profit, to a system of key account management (KAM).

In KAM, the supplier assesses the true cost, and therefore profitability, of doing business with a particular customer for a specified product or service. In addition to the direct costs of production, all other expenses incurred in winning and retaining the business are calculated and aggregated. Included in the calculation are an appropriate share of overheads, together with the costs of sales visits, provision of promotional materials, special quality and service requirements, the effort involved in responding to problems and other special buyer demands, and entertainment. When total costs compiled in this way are set against sales realizations, the profitability of each piece of business becomes evident, and so, therefore, does its attractiveness.

Sales organizations will then use this information to decide on strategies to be applied in interacting with their customer base. Such strategies would range from vigorous defence, through maintenance and development, to selective withdrawal. Decisions on the strategy to be employed will be subject to the supplier's perception of the overall attractiveness of the business relationship as described later (see also 'Procurement marketing' in Chapter 8). The decision matrix is represented graphically in Fig 6.1[1].

This figure plots the attractiveness of the customer (Y axis) against the competitive position of the supplier (X axis). Attractiveness is principally profitability but also includes other features such as a real opportunity for growth, beneficial association with a high-profile name, acquisition of technical or other knowledge, and the certainty of prompt payment. These factors are described in more detail as the procurement marketing concept. The competitive position is an assessment of the ability of the supplier to compete for that business in that market. This would include the existence of a technical advantage, a superior logistics chain (location, etc.), and a highly supportive marketing network.

From Fig. 6.1 it can be seen that when the competitive position is strong and the attractiveness is high then the supplier's strategy will be to defend and if possible develop the business. This will greatly influence both attitude and response to demands made by the customer, including

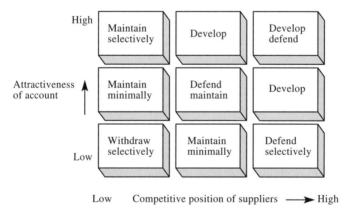

Fig. 6.1 Strategic options for key accounts

a willingness to change and innovate. Conversely, when the attractiveness is low and the competitive position is weak, then the supplier is likely to adopt a strategy involving selective withdrawal. This may be disguised in some other form (such as apparent inability to meet standards) and may take place over a considerable period of time.

Figure 6.1 also shows that suppliers may adopt other intermediate strategies dependent on where the customer is positioned in the matrix. It is therefore important for purchasers to determine as far as is possible how their business is perceived by the supplier. This can best be achieved as a coordinated multi-functional activity, including visits to the supplier and discussions with as many of the supplier's staff as possible. Purchasers should not rely on a direct approach to get the true response.

Customer segmentation by suppliers

At this stage it may be helpful to consider another way in which a supplier could set up their market segmentation analysis. In this case, the supplier would plot the attractiveness of customer accounts against the relative value of the business (as a function of total sales) in the manner shown in Fig. 6.2.

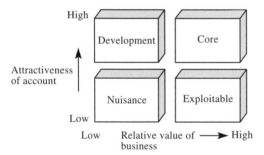

Fig. 6.2 Market segmentation by the supplier

As with the supply positioning model, a four box analysis has been used to define strategies and for convenience these boxes have been given labels as follows:

- nuisance
- development
- exploitable
- core.

NUISANCE

Nuisance includes those items which are of relatively low value and where the account is in any case not very attractive. In this case the supplier might be expected to show little interest and support and to be actively making efforts to withdraw.

DEVELOPMENT

Development includes those items which, although being of relatively low value, nevertheless form an account which is attractive to the supplier. An example of this might be where a supplier has gained a small toehold with a 'blue chip' customer and sees the opportunity to gain more valuable business at some future date by virtue of this relationship. In this situation the supplier may be expected to work hard, at least in the short term, to meet and exceed the requirements of the customer in order to win more business.

EXPLOITABLE

In the exploitable sector the supplier may have a high volume of sales, which forms a substantial part of the business, in an account which is not regarded as very attractive. The reason for this could be that the business is not truly profitable or that the supplier is required to operate under unfavourable or uncertain conditions due to location, or other factors.

Although the loss of this account might result in spare capacity in the short term, there will be considerable pressure to increase margins and consequently prices to compensate for some of the above factors. In this situation the supplier may be expected to be trying to drive maximum short-term benefit to cover this inconvenience; this would be manifested by steeply rising prices and frequent requests for other value-added features. Overall, the supplier will not be too concerned about losing the customer because of these actions.

CORE

The core is of high value in an attractive account. The supplier will regard this as the bedrock of the business portfolio and would be most concerned if it were lost or reduced in any way. The supplier may be expected to provide these customers with a high level of service and attention and to be seeking every means of ensuring the business is retained while seeking to increase profitability in a low profile manner. Such a supplier is likely to be receptive to suggestions of strategic alliance and other ways of locking-in to the customer. These overall supplier's objectives are summarized in Figs 6.3, 6.4, 6.5 and 6.6.

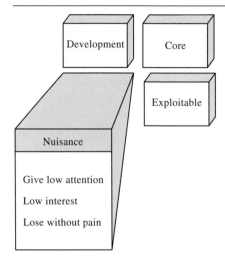

Fig. 6.3 Supplier objectives: nuisance category

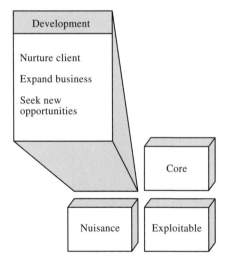

Fig. 6.4 Supplier objectives: development category

Matching supply positioning with customer segmentation

If we now match supply positioning by buyers with customer segmentation by suppliers, we can deduce whether the appropriate supplier has been selected for any element of business and what synergies, or

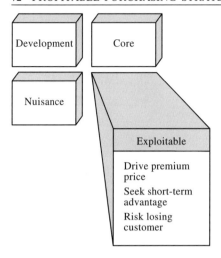

Fig. 6.5 Supplier objectives: exploitable category

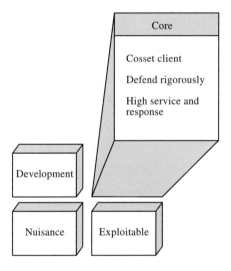

Fig. 6.6 Supplier objectives: core category

otherwise, might exist. We shall do this by considering each of the supply positioning quadrants in turn and evaluating the impact of the supplier's potential response on the overall procurement objectives which have previously been suggested.

TACTICAL ACQUISITION

With those low risk, low cost items, the buyer's strategy is to minimize the attention required and drive for efficiency in the procurement process. Often this will be achieved by setting up long-term contracts with a high service element and effectively handing the responsibility over to a supplier.

If this represents **core** business for the supplier then a very good result may be expected since the supplier will work hard and give a great deal of attention to something with which the buying organization does not want to be too concerned. Since costs to the purchasing organization are low, the supplier will be able to achieve good margins without impacting on the profitability of the buyer.

A similar outcome may be expected if the supplier identifies the business as being in the **development** category, but in this instance the buyer may eventually have to start to offer additional incentives (such as supplementary business) in order to retain commitment in the longer term.

Problems arise when the supplier identifies this business as being in either the **nuisance** or **exploitable** categories.

In the case of the nuisance, neither the supplier nor the buyer will wish to put in much effort and the buying organization may find itself continually having to resolve problems and overcome difficulties associated with trivial non-strategic purchases. There is clearly a mismatch between buyer and seller resulting from low energy and interest and in this situation the buyer must seriously consider finding an alternate supplier with a better segmentation fit.

If a supplier classifies this business as exploitable the supplier will be motivated to continue with it, provided it becomes profitable. In this situation the buyer can afford to allow a certain amount of price rises in return for heightened or expanding services. The buyer will need to monitor long-term service trends, and be prepared to change suppliers if a stable outcome is not realized.

Figures 6.7, 6.8, 6.9 and 6.10 summarize the overall situation and the buyer's desirable response for tactical acquisition items in these four categories.

STRATEGIC SECURITY

Strategic security (low cost, high risk) items call for considerable supplier support and commitment. The buyer is seeking to ensure supply by setting up long-term contracts. Price is not a major factor in the considerations.

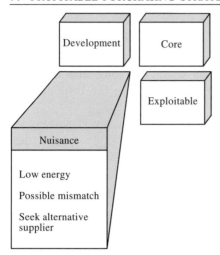

Fig. 6.7 Buyer's response for tactical acquisition items: nuisance category

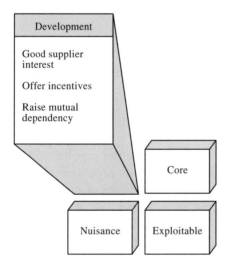

Fig. 6.8 Buyer's response for tactical acquisition items: development category

As with tactical acquisition, if the supplier regards this as **core** business then a good match will ensue and both parties should be content to enter into long-term contractual arrangements and indeed develop closer relations, thus providing the buyer with the supply security that is desired.

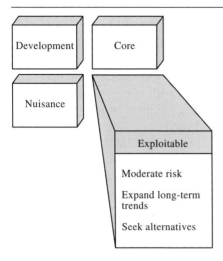

Fig. 6.9 Buyer's response for tactical acquisition: exploitable category

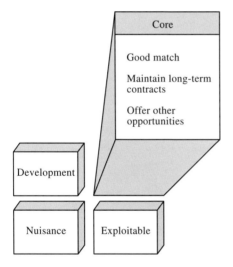

Fig. 6.10 Buyer's response for tactical acquisition: core category

If the supplier sees the business as **development**, then the supplier will be motivated by future potential rather than the immediate benefits. The buyer must therefore work hard to increase mutual dependency so that the supplier increases commitment and becomes more 'locked-in' to the relationship.

If the supplier categorizes the business as **nuisance** then the buying organization is in a *very* high risk situation particularly with regard to desired service. There is a real danger that the supplier could lose interest and in some circumstances cease production. Every effort should be made to change to a more compatible supplier. Since this may not always be possible, it may be necessary to alleviate the situation by offering additional incentives such as extra business of another type or even higher prices in return for improved services.

Where the supplier categorizes this item as **exploitable**, the buyer is in a moderate risk situation mostly associated with cost. However, since cost is not a principal consideration in the strategic security segment, the buyer may assume that the relationship can be maintained provided that changes are made to increase the attractiveness of the account to the supplier. This may be in the form of increased prices or other benefits. Buyers will need to closely monitor service and ultimately be prepared, if possible, to change suppliers if high standards are not maintained.

Figures 6.11, 6.12, 6.13 and 6.14 illustrate the overall situation and the buyer's best response when dealing with strategic security items.

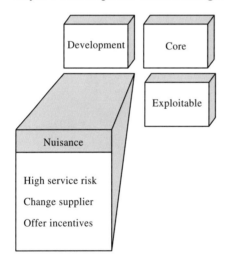

Fig. 6.11   Buyer's response for strategic security items: nuisance category

TACTICAL PROFIT

The prime motivation of the buyer is to drive for profit, exploiting the market as appropriate.

As in all cases where the supplier regards the business as **core**, there will be considerable commitment because the objectives of both buyer

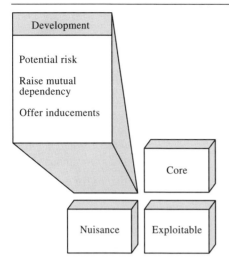

Fig. 6.12 Buyer's response for strategic security items: development category

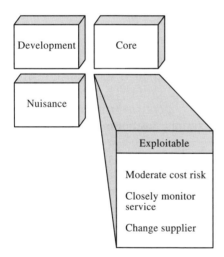

Fig. 6.13 Buyer's response for strategic security items: exploitable category

and seller are compatible although not the same. The objective of the supplier will be to seek longer-term contracts while the buyer will usually wish to keep them short term. Also the buyer is in an excellent position from which to drive profit contribution because the buyer is operating in a relatively easy market with the availability of competition. However, in order to avoid 'turning off' the supplier a wise

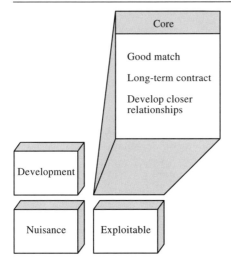

Fig. 6.14 Buyer's response for strategic security items: core category

buyer would seek ways to encourage continued participation and interest.

Buyers should also consider whether further commercial advantage can be obtained by treating certain cases as though they fall into the strategic critical category rather than tactical profit. That implies being prepared to enter into longer-term, more cooperative arrangements than is indicated by strict application of the supply positioning guidelines for tactical profit.

Participation should also be encouraged where the supplier classifies the business as **development** as this represents an excellent way in which the buyer can increase and develop competition in the marketplace.

If the supplier classifies the business as **nuisance** then this is a clear mismatch. However, it may be possible to accept this because the relationship will, in any case, be short term. In the end it is likely that the buyer will change suppliers or that the supplier will withdraw from any arrangement.

Where a tactical profit item for the buyer is also an **exploitable** item for the seller, then both parties are focusing on price as a means of driving their own profit. They are therefore likely to be cast in an adversarial role, negotiating within a confined 'price tunnel'. Buyers should approach such suppliers with great care, tightly controlling the release of information and seeking competition wherever possible. In these circumstances it is most unlikely that a lasting or profitable relationship can develop.

Figures 6.15, 6.16, 6.17 and 6.18 summarize the overall position and the buyer's best responses when acquiring tactical profit items.

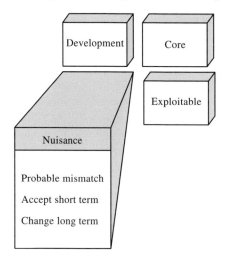

Fig. 6.15 Buyer's response for tactical profit items: nuisance category

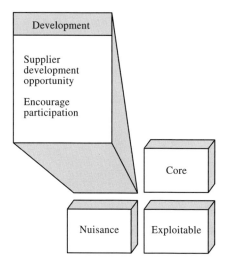

Fig. 6.16 Buyer's response for tactical profit items: development category

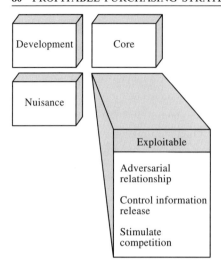

Fig. 6.17   Buyer's response for tactical profit items: exploitable category

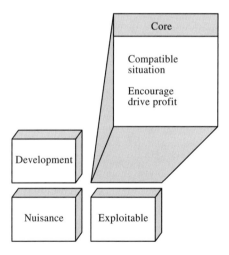

Fig. 6.18   Buyer's response for tactical profit items: core category

STRATEGIC CRITICAL

The overall objective of the buyer is to closely monitor seller performance and to work to enhance relationships.

In the case where the supplier sees this business as **core** it may be considered that there is a good buyer–supplier match which should be developed and encouraged; it is in this situation that partnerships or strategic alliances are most likely to flourish.

Where the business is classified as **development**, the buyer should work closely with the supplier to increase the extent and content of the business; this may involve seeking out other categories of business in which both have a mutual interest.

The juxtaposition of strategic critical with either **nuisance** or **exploitable** should be a cause for concern. Strategic critical items are essential to the success of the buyer's business and problems with either supply or pricing cannot be accepted. A change of supplier is indicated; however, given that it may not be possible, the buyer will have to devote considerable time and attention to this supply situation. In the case of the nuisance category, the buyer should try to make the business relationship more attractive and so provide the supplier with a greater incentive to continue to do business in an economic manner. In the case of the exploitable category, the buyer should try to raise the level of mutual dependency making it unattractive for the supplier to act in an adversarial manner.

Figures 6.19, 6.20, 6.21 and 6.22 summarize the overall situation for the buyer's best response for strategic critical items.

Summary

Supply positioning (see Chapter 5) can be viewed as a logical evolutionary outcome of applying analytical methods—such as pioneered by Pareto—to provide the degree of professional management of bought-in resources demanded by the best leading-edge concerns today.

Positioning, however, does not stand alone; in this chapter equal weight has been given to examining the suppliers' preferred modes of undertaking what is, essentially, a similar analysis of best methods for fulfilling commercial aims and objectives to achieve strategic success. The complementary nature of Chapters 5 and 6 describe well-researched and thought-provoking measures which represent a quantum leap away from the perception of the adversarial cultures of yesteryear. Ways of attaining commercial convergence will be further explored in succeeding chapters.

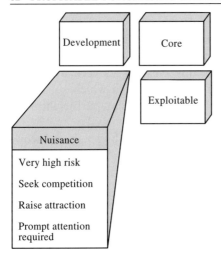

Fig. 6.19   Buyer's response for strategic critical items: nuisance category

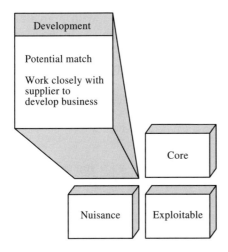

Fig. 6.20   Buyer's response for strategic critical items: development category

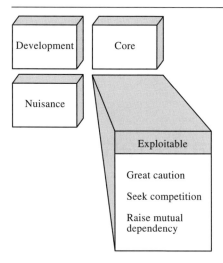

Fig. 6.21 Buyer's response for strategic critical items: exploitable category

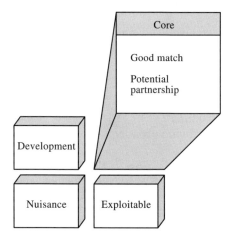

Fig. 6.22 Buyer's response for strategic critical items: core category

Notes and references

1 Burnett, K. (1992) *Strategic Customer Alliances*, Pitman, London.

7

Vulnerability management

Chapters 5 and 6 described two of the elements of supply planning activity—supply positioning and supplier preferences—designed to establish the current market position with regard to a supply item. The way in which these fit together was outlined in Fig. 3.3 which is reproduced as Fig. 7.1.

In this chapter we shall turn our attention to vulnerability management, which is the third element used to determine the current market position.

A prime task of an effective purchasing function is always to provide the business with a secure supply situation irrespective of the forces that may be operating in the macro environment. Fire, earthquake, flood, strike, sinking boats, etc., still do not provide an adequate excuse for a failure of the supply lines.

Many organizations fail to give proper attention to this factor, thus exposing the business to considerable supply-side risks. Here are two examples:

- A high quality printing operation made use of a relatively low cost product whose purpose was to keep the print rollers clean and at the same time recover surplus ink for reuse. It was discovered that there was only one supplier; a very small factory owned by a gentleman in his seventies. Further investigation showed that there was no one who could take over the business when the present owner ceased to be interested or available. The print works was thus exposed to the real possibility that supply of a crucial, albeit low cost, item could cease without warning, possibly shutting down the whole operation.
- A manufacturer of household goods discovered that a vital component

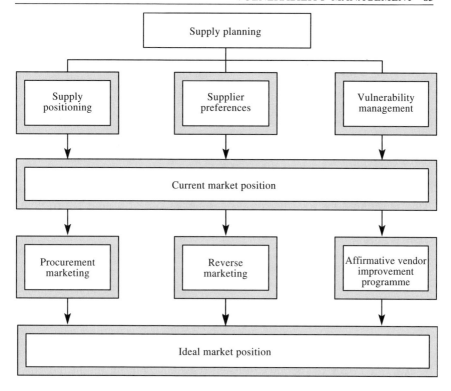

Fig. 7.1   Supply planning model

of its leading brand was manufactured by the sole supplier using a very unstable and somewhat dangerous process. Again there was a real possibility that a factory incident could result in severe loss of production with the manufacturer being unable to sell a product contributing a very high proportion of income and profit.

In a high-performing purchasing environment, vulnerability management is an important activity and, as can be seen from the two examples, in some instances will be crucial to the ongoing success of the business. The application of a sound process in this area will identify business vulnerabilities and enable some very creative solutions, which minimize risk, to be put into place.

To ensure that all areas have been considered, it will be necessary for purchasing personnel to lead a multi-functional team through a structured approach to the analysis of issues that could affect the integrity of the supply line. Once the analysis is undertaken, a prioritization of the issues requiring rectification can be agreed, and specific action planning put in place.

Identifying vulnerabilities

Vulnerability analysis and management are time-consuming activities and therefore cannot be applied to all purchases. The use of the supply positioning technique will assist purchasers in selecting those goods and services which are of the most significance to a buying organization. It is probable that the candidates for this analysis will be categorized as strategic security or strategic critical. However, there may well be some items in tactical profit which might benefit from a similar approach. Among the reasons for this could be the existence of potential problems further up the supply chain, or market distortions such as cartels or self-created monopolies.

In each case it is important to ensure that the entire supply chain is examined and that analysis is not confined to the first-level suppliers, otherwise many potential problems could be missed. This involves assessing the activities of the first-level suppliers, then determining the items which they purchase, applying the same analysis on their suppliers and so on until reaching the raw-material stage.

For example, in the case of cardboard cartons, the supply chain could be examined back to the harvesting of trees. The output might therefore be as follows:

Commodity	folding cartons
Supplier	J. Smith & Co.
Annual spend	£3.5 million
Supply positioning	tactical profit

The supply chain would be as shown in Fig. 7.2. At each stage a supply positioning analysis and a market analysis would be undertaken. The result of this might demonstrate that activity in this chain falls into more than one supply positioning category. For example, conversion to cartons might be tactical profit whereas the supply of pulp might be classified as strategic critical requiring a totally different management approach.

In performing the supply-chain assessment, an examination of the logistics between each process should also be made and vulnerabilities identified. When doing this analysis, for example, one client in Latin America discovered that the key item in the chain was the logistics of moving goods from Venezuela to Brazil, and that only one boat per

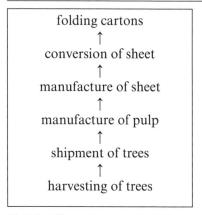

folding cartons
↑
conversion of sheet
↑
manufacture of sheet
↑
manufacture of pulp
↑
shipment of trees
↑
harvesting of trees

Fig 7.2   The cartons supply chain

month was available and capable of performing the task; thus the delivery became long overdue if the supplier missed the boat.

Considerations such as given here become especially critical when considering items which at some stage in the chain are affected by commodity markets or are subject to global, political, or climatic changes. Examples are the impact of the cotton crop on the demand for Methyl Ethyl Glycol or frost in California impacting on the world supply–demand balance for orange juice. Also, it is not so long ago that the supply-side was rocked by a huge hike in oil prices and acute shortages in paper products.

Regular undertaking of such analyses, as dictated by demand, helps the purchasing function to focus on global economic issues, identify potential problems, and take pre-emptive steps to avoid their worst effects. In this way buyers provide their organizations with another competitive edge.

There are seven main areas where vulnerability might be assessed:

- supply–demand balance
- raw-materials availability
- raw-materials cost trends
- rate of technical innovation
- complexity of the market
- the supplier
- production, shipping, and distribution methods.

These vulnerable areas will now be discussed:

SUPPLY–DEMAND BALANCE

There would need to be an evaluation of the buyer's requirement as a percentage of market, the buyer's requirement as a percentage of supplier's production, the risk of shortages, the effect of other buyers in the market, overall volumes, and future requirements when set against availability.

RAW-MATERIALS AVAILABILITY

Further up the supply chain there should also be concern about the supplier's own source of raw-materials, including location, certainty of supplier continuation, and other issues. This would include the nature of the raw-materials, their source, the potential for supply disruption due to political instability or delivery through an unstable area, and the risk of natural disasters.

RAW-MATERIALS COST TRENDS

In this category it would be necessary to examine trends over past years, information concerning the price outlook for the product, and events or developments likely to trigger substantial cost increases.

RATE OF TECHNICAL INNOVATION

Here it will be necessary to take account of the frequency of new ideas or concepts, the life cycle of the product, and emerging technology in order to assess the probability of continued availability or the product being superseded.

COMPLEXITY OF THE MARKET

This would include determining the existence of cartels, the relative strengths of buyer(s) and supplier, and whether suppliers are prevented from entering the market due to inter-supplier agreements or government regulations.

THE SUPPLIER

In this category it will be necessary to consider aspects covering finance, marketplace behaviour, and management attitude.

Among the financial considerations would be the trends in profitability and cashflow and the existence or not of parent company guarantees.

Marketplace behaviour would include the pricing policy pursued, price trends compared to inflation, willingness to discount, and the price compared to competitors. Other factors to take into account would be the supplier's share of the product market, whether the company is an influencer or follower, and the extent to which it is a monopoly supplier.

Many potential problems can be overcome if the supplier management have the right attitude. It is necessary to establish whether there is sufficient openness and trust, together with a willingness to continually seek change and improvement.

PRODUCTION, SHIPPING, AND DISTRIBUTION METHODS
It will be most important to fully understand the production method, including whether it has severe safety or environmental implications, whether it is a batch or continuous process, retooling time, and economic minimum quantities. It will be necessary to understand the production location and whether there is flexibility to manufacture at alternative sites.

It will also be worth while to evaluate the methods by which the product is distributed, whether there are any special handling or storage problems, and whether there are any special packaging problems.

When working through the vulnerability analysis there will be a temptation to make use of some form of checklist. This should be avoided, since experience has shown that checklists seem to inhibit entrepreneurial thinking, so essential in this exercise.

Assessing the risk
To arrive at a prioritized list of areas requiring attention, the following filters should be applied to any given potential area of risk:

- probability of the event occurring
- likely duration of the problem
- impact on the business.

PROBABILITY OF THE EVENT OCCURRING
Using some form of probability analysis it should be possible to predict the chances of the occurrence of any event into the three broad categories of high, medium, or low. Analysts can make their own definitions of these categories but a suggestion is as follows:

High probability

High probability would apply where there has been experience of an identical or broadly similar problem in the past, for example, if the manufacturing process is known to have a certain instability and there have been supply interruptions in the past due to process failure of one kind or another. It might also apply where there are observed trends which could create an as yet unencountered problem, for example, a deterioration in the political stability of a source country.

Medium probability

Medium probability would apply to those situations where there would appear to be inherent difficulties but which have not yet manifested themselves in a supply interruption. In these cases small changes in circumstances might be enough to create a supply problem.

Low probability

Low probability category would include those situations which, while not beyond the realms of possibility, are most unlikely to occur in all reasonable scenarios.

LIKELY DURATION OF THE PROBLEM

In most cases some estimate can be made based upon statistical analysis of past experience. For example, when in the early 1980s industrial relations problems in the UK were very significant, clear statistical patterns could be seen, which, when extrapolated, gave a very good indication of what might be expected for the future. The study led to the implementation of defensive actions which enabled buying companies to continue manufacture irrespective of the industrial relations difficulties of suppliers. Here the outcome of the analysis was a view expressed as the number of working days that the problem would be likely to exist.

IMPACT ON THE BUSINESS

Detailed discussion is likely to be needed between the various members of a multi-functional team in order to quantify the size of the issue and its effect on the profitability of the business. For example, a company might deduce that after two weeks without production, the supply to customers would begin to fail. Every percentage point drop in sales performance would hit short-term profit by a certain amount. Longer term, the risk is loss of the sole source status with the key accounts, thus putting at risk a high percentage of the volume and substantial annual profits.

Managing the risk

Once all these three 'filters' are completed, it becomes possible to identify and quantify the risks. In turn this highlights the priority areas in specific products and markets that have the greatest potential to damage the future health of the business. It is now possible to commence developing risk management plans for the most serious cases. In developing such plans, buyers will need to constantly balance risks versus the costs of eliminating them. There is no point in overburdening an organization with contingency plans which are so expensive that they cripple the business financially.

As this is a three-dimensional problem (probability, duration, impact) it is recommended that buyers prioritize the areas for attention in line with the three matrices illustrated in Figs 7.3 (high probability), 7.4 (medium probability), and 7.5 (low probability). Within these figures each category is ranked from 1 to 12, with 1–4 being the first areas for attention.

ACTION FOR HIGH PROBABILITY

For those areas where the risk is defined as having a high probability of occurring, recommended action is as shown in Fig. 7.3.

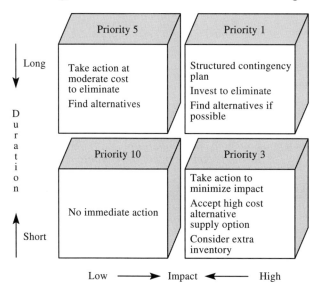

Fig. 7.3   Action for high probability risk

In this figure a combination of high probability, long duration, and high business impact is labelled as Priority 1 requiring urgent and comprehensive action. In this case, buyers would be justified in developing a structured contingency plan which could include investment to eliminate the problem. Alternatives should be found if at all possible.

For Priority 3 it will be seen that, while a structured contingency plan might not be justified, action to eliminate should be taken provided it is of moderate cost. Since the predicted duration is short, it may be acceptable to rely on an alternative method of temporary supply even though it is of high cost. Here again, alternatives should be actively sought.

For Priority 5, it is unlikely that major investment can be justified although action should be taken if it is of moderate cost. The search for alternatives should continue. It is of course recognized that such actions either may not be possible or may be too expensive. In which case buyers, together with interested parties from other functions, will need to consider the problem as a whole, weighing up vulnerability against the other factors.

In contrast, in Priority 10, even though there is still high probability, duration is short and impact is low and it is therefore not necessary to take immediate action.

ACTION FOR MEDIUM PROBABILITY

Recommended action for medium probability items is illustrated in Fig. 7.4.

In areas of medium probability there will be cause for concern only where the impact on the business is high. In the case of both long and short duration, corrective action is recommended if at all possible. Where the impact is low, action is recommended only where duration is predicted to be high.

Thus Priority 2 requires the same approach as Priority 1, calling for investment and a structured contingency plan. For Priority 4, major investment cannot be justified but low cost defensive action is required as well as the continued search for alternatives. It will be acceptable to rely on a high cost alternative supply option in the event of a problem.

With Priority 7, it will be acceptable to rely on a high cost alternative supply option in the event of a problem. Low cost actions to minimize duration should also be considered. No action is required in relation to Priority 11.

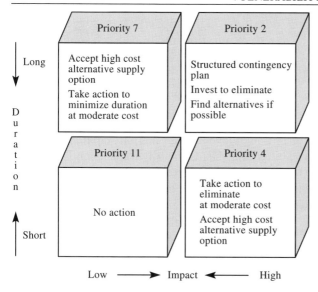

Fig. 7.4 Action for medium probability risk

ACTION FOR LOW PROBABILITY

Turning attention now to areas where there is a low probability, recommended action is as illustrated in Fig. 7.5.

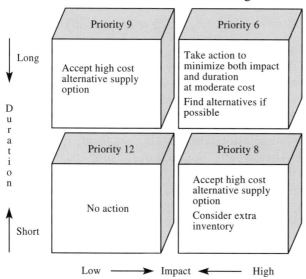

Fig. 7.5 Action for low probability risk

For Priority 6 (long duration, high impact) it is suggested that moderate cost solutions to reduce duration and impact are sought.

In all other cases of low probability the recommendation is that little or no immediate action is required and in the case of low impact virtually none at all.

Vulnerability analysis

There is clearly going to be a high level of supplier participation involved in undertaking a vulnerability analysis. Generally it has been found that an open approach with suppliers is the most beneficial, often resulting in very fast remedial action. In the worked example shown in the next section the supplier was taken through the analysis, quickly identified the issues, and put in place relatively simple remedies to eliminate the problem. The supplier became more motivated through being assisted by the buying organization to identify a problem, put in place a remedy, and improve profitability by reduced downtime.

To summarize, solutions *must* be kept as simple as possible because few organizations can afford the luxury of many weeks and much cost in eliminating problems. There is no point in overburdening an organization with contingency plans which are so complex and expensive to implement that they almost cripple the business financially.

A worked example

A worked example is shown in Fig. 7.6, which relates to the supply of a chemical component.

Three potential areas of vulnerability have been identified:

- fire or explosion at the supplier
- delivery failure
- quality problems with the supplier's manufacturing process.

The probability of fire or explosion is rated as high as the manufacturing process is rather risky. The potential duration of the problem is variable from one or two days to three or four months depending on the severity of the incident. The impact on the business is severe, in the worst case destroying sales and market position. Overall, because of a combination of high probability, lengthy duration, and severe impact, the problem is given a priority of 1.

Proposed actions in this case include reviewing the nature of the manufacturing process with the supplier with the aim of minimizing the risk both short and long term. In one real-life case, short-term action involved getting the supplier to relocate the finished product tank away

Risk management analysis sheet

Product	Chemical hyperacton					
Potential vulnerability	Probability of occurrence	Duration of problem	Impact on the business	Ranking of priority	Proposed action	Target completion date
Fire or explosion at the supplier	High-manufacturing process for this chemical is risky	Variable 1–2 days at best 3–4 months at worst	Severe in the worst case Could destroy sales of the product	1	Review process with supplier to minimize risk Investigate alternative materials with lower risk Investigate alternative supply sources	Immediate Q1 1995 Q2 1995 if above actions fail
Delivery failure	Medium/low	Past record indicates occasional supply failures Worst case 4 days late	Little/no impact	11/12	Review supply performance with supplier and agree programme to improve to 100% on time	Next meeting with the supplier Regular monitor
Quality problem with supplier's manufacturing process	Medium	Best 2–3 days Worst 2 months	Severe impact could destroy product reputation	2	Review entire manufacturing quality process controls Agree any changes Progress implementation	Next 10 working days As above To progress target complete all within 6 months

Fig. 7.6 Vulnerability analysis: a worked example

from the immediate vicinity of the process thus protecting up to 20 days' stock. Longer term, both parties should investigate the possibility of alternative products or processes and the buyer should evaluate alternative or additional sources.

The probability of delivery failure is estimated as medium to low because the past record indicates only occasional supply failures, the worst case being four days late. This is perceived as having little or no impact on the business and therefore the potential risk is ranked as 11 or 12 overall. Remedial action is therefore low key and included as part of the regular buyer–supplier interaction.

The probability of encountering quality problems with the supplier's manufacturing process is estimated as medium, based on past experience where there has been little to report. Should a quality problem emerge it is estimated that it could last at the best for two to three days and at worst for up to two months. However, the potential impact is very severe in that it could destroy the product reputation; for this reason the risk is given a high ranking of 2. This stimulates the buying organization to take preventive action thus moving the whole activity from the reactive to the proactive.

Remedial action includes a review of the entire manufacturing process with particular emphasis on quality assurance and quality control. Such a review is a joint buyer–supplier activity which will be completed in a reasonable time and will result in joint implementation of identified changes.

In this example, a detailed appraisal of the key issues would need to be carried out in a very open manner with the supplier's senior management and at their manufacturing location. The product would be a specific, focused, time-bounded, action plan which would be reviewed at frequent intervals in order to

● make sure the agreed changes are implemented in a timely manner
● ensure the discipline is sustained over time.

The goal which should always remain in focus is :

> *To make a substantial reduction in the risk exposure in a short period of time and then to sustain at that level, or preferably lower the risk in the medium term.*

Once the analysis is complete, and the actions needed to resolve the risk are taken, a record of the analysis, the action plan, and the results of the implementation of the action plan, should be maintained in the commodity file, in order to assist future reviews.

The position on vulnerability, once it has been resolved, should be reconsidered if:

- supply-market forces change (e.g. new entrant)
- take-overs occur
- there is a new use for the material
- new customers enter the market
- supplier plans to implement technology or manufacturing process changes
- buyer's market position strengthens
- buyer extends the range of the product via new launches etc.

This is a powerful process and, used effectively, will not only reduce vulnerability, but also enhance the image of the company with its suppliers. A further consequence will be that the vulnerability management technique will be seen very positively by the suppliers and will be another step in the quest to be considered as a 'preferred customer' (see Chapter 8).

Cost reduction

It is not unusual, when undertaking a vulnerability analysis exercise, suddenly to stumble upon a substantial opportunity to influence and reduce costs dramatically as a side benefit.

When we have no choice but to take action on a procurement problem, we are forced to re-examine the basic need and the various ways in which this need can be satisfactorily met. Such a systematic approach to need definitions and its satisfaction almost invariably yields better results than the original design or specification.

(Leenders and Blenkhorn 1988)[1]
(as quoted from work undertaken by Larry Miles in 1948)

This is particularly true when the item in question sits high in the strategic critical box of the supply positioning analysis. Here, because the market, by definition, is difficult, margins are generally high and the suppliers often complacent. Vulnerability analysis, combined with other tools covered elsewhere in this book, has resulted in significant gains for many organizations.

For example, on a key raw material in the strategic critical box, one company, having discovered how vulnerable it was, implemented a change programme that not only reduced the vulnerability but also delivered a substantial competitive edge because of a major saving (25 per cent) in total cost. Until the vulnerability analysis was undertaken the conventional wisdom was that there were few problems and that in any case there was nothing that could be done.

Other issues to consider
- Beware of developing voluminous checklists which require people to place ticks in boxes. This approach has an irritating habit of switching off people's brains! The consequence is that while the focus is on completion of the checklist, the goal of ensuring that all vulnerabilities are covered might be missed (especially if a key vulnerability is not on the checklist).
- Analyses and the development of potential solutions are best done by multi-functional teams, with at least one team member being totally unfamiliar with the product; this should ensure that even the obvious issues are explored rather than ignored.
- Do not try and analyse too many areas at once. Fix the ones that will bring the greatest relief to those people in the organization who are accountable for sales and profit performance. (Fix the rest as soon as is practical, once the big vulnerabilities are removed.)
- Initial focus should be via supply positioning, into the two strategic boxes, where, by definition, the markets are difficult. At a later stage consider the tactical profit box, although vulnerability here should be unlikely if the market is being managed in line with the recommended actions for that box.
- Having extra sources of supply approved does not necessarily reduce vulnerability. It is possible to be in a potentially far stronger position by finding solutions with existing suppliers, rather than diluting effort by pursuing a dual or triple option, which could take much time, focus, and cost, to arrange.

Summary
We have now completed the discussion on the three techniques—supply positioning, supplier preferences, and vulnerability management—which enable buyers to define the nature of the current supply market. With vulnerability management we have moved on to consider moves that can be made to change the market to the buyer's advantage. We shall consider this issue in more depth in Chapter 8.

Notes and references
1 Leenders, M. R. and Blenkhorn, D. L. (1988) *Reverse Marketing*, The Free Press, Maxwell Macmillan, Ontario, Canada.

8

Influencing the supply-market

Chapters 4 to 7 represent the first stage of the supply planning process outlined in Chapter 3. Chapter 4 provided insights into the true nature of the supply-market and Chapters 5 to 7 provided details of the techniques that can be used to determine and evaluate the current market position. However, effective buyers will seek to influence and change the supply-market to their advantage; this chapter describes three techniques which can be used. These are procurement marketing, reverse marketing, and affirmative vendor improvement. Figure 3.3 showed how the techniques link together and is reproduced as Fig. 8.1.

Procurement marketing is designed to change the perception of the buyer in the supplier's mind, thus allowing the buyer to gain advantage. Reverse marketing is about creating a supply capability where either one does not exist or the market is distorted. Affirmative vendor improvement is a technique used to help suppliers upgrade their performance.

Procurement marketing

A proposal that organizations should devote time and attention to make themselves a 'favoured buyer' for a supplier may at first seem a rather odd concept to put to purchasing managers and buyers. It is in direct contrast to the conventional wisdom that it is up to the supplier to compete for business and to design and offer products that meet buyers' needs. In this scenario the buyer is cast in a relatively passive role waiting to reap the benefits of frantic competitive activity in the supply-market.

CHANGES IN THE MARKETPLACE
While this approach may have been appropriate in the past, there have been many important changes in the marketplace which should make

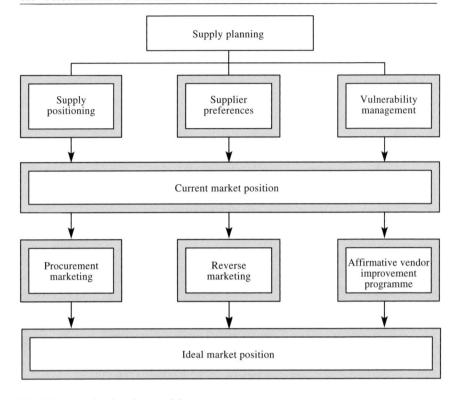

Fig. 8.1 Supply planning model

forward-looking buying organizations re-evaluate the position. Among these changes are the following.

- The shift of emphasis within sales organizations causing them to move from volume-related targets to key account management. In the latter scenario each customer is carefully evaluated to determine the net contribution that it makes to the corporate profit of the seller. All costs in serving the account (sales visits, promotional support, payment practices, etc.) are accrued and set against income.
- Only those customers delivering or having the potential to deliver strong profit streams will be targeted. The remainder will face high price increases or even disinterest. (Key account management was discussed in Chapter 6.)
- It is likely that in certain market segments the number of suppliers may reduce considerably and that those that remain will be larger and may start to be more discriminating in the selection of their trading partners.

- The increase in bought-out materials and services as a percentage of sales revenue. For most manufacturing organizations this is now in excess of 60 per cent and for some it is as high as 80 per cent. Even for non-manufacturing companies the level is now reaching 30–40 per cent.
- Shorter product life cycles limiting opportunities to use such techniques as value analysis as a way of reducing costs. Typically life cycles which used to be measured in years can now be measured in months.
- The increasingly frequent need to source outside of a particular locality, country, or continent with consequent greatly lengthened lines of communication.

Even without these, it has always been true that many potentially excellent suppliers have often been discouraged from bidding for business because of the posture and image of the buying organization. Massive and complicated documentation at the enquiry or tender stage together with detailed contractual terms that are clearly too onerous are just some of the reasons for this reaction. The net effect is to limit the market artificially and put the buyer at a serious disadvantage for certain segments of the buying portfolio.

Therefore it is time to look afresh at buyer–seller relationships. It is, of course, true that there has always been a high interest in this area, but whereas there is a mountain of literature and information aimed at aiding marketers, little attention has been given to encouraging buyers to 'sell' to suppliers on the benefits of doing business with them. Nor has much attention been given to the value of organized efforts to attract certain suppliers, specifically by adopting purchasing policies that help the buying organization to position itself advantageously in the supply-market.

In selectively targeted instances we believe that buyers can make their organizations be seen by suppliers as a 'favoured customer'.

Anyone who has studied marketing will know that focusing on the customer is central to the marketing function. Marketeers aim to generate customer satisfaction and by doing so satisfy their own organizational goals.

There have been a great many marketing-based studies into buyer behaviour where preferences of buyers for suppliers have been evaluated and the learning used to develop the marketing/sales approach.

In contrast there has been little work done on examining the selling procedures and approaches of sellers in order to develop knowledge and understanding of these that would be helpful to purchasing.

From the work that has been done, and our own studies, we can

COSUMNES RIVER COLLEGE
LEARNING RESOURCE CENTER

conclude that suppliers as well as buyers have preferences with respect to those with whom they wish to deal. Just as it is with buyers, sellers use these preferences to allocate their resources in certain segments of their markets. This was reflected in Fig. 6.2.

Among the resources that suppliers could allocate to their customers we can include:

- quality and quantity of products and services
- research and development and technical services
- credit
- distribution services including mode and timing of shipments and containerization
- assumption of various inventory functions
- provision of market information.

In certain segments of a market, buyers may have to compete for these valuable resources. To do so in an effective way buyers need to understand the preferences of suppliers, just as the marketing functions of the suppliers must focus on the needs and preferences of the buyers.

THE PROCUREMENT MARKETING CONCEPT

If this similarity is accepted, one can apply the marketing concept to the procurement function. This is why we call it the procurement marketing concept.

This concept requires purchasing managers and buyers to re-examine strategies and tactics for certain segments of the market. It calls for an orientation toward the supplier with the aim of obtaining upward movement along the Y axis of the supplier's decision matrix, denoting enhanced attractiveness of the account to the seller (see Fig. 6.1) and so generating new interest by the desired supplier, in the buying organization.

In this way the goals of the buying concern are helped in a difficult supply-market situation.

METHODS OF ATTRACTING SUPPLIERS

Given that it has been decided to apply the concept, it is now necessary to consider how to go about it. This means asking the question 'What attributes is a favoured buyer likely to have?' This may well come down to the policies of the buying organization.

Among those attributes likely to attract suppliers will be the following.

- The prospect of ongoing profitable business. Whereas suppliers are sometimes willing to trade at prices close to their marginal costs, it is rarely that they would wish such prices to be the basis of a long-term contract.
- The certainty of prompt payment according to the contractual terms. With many accounts departments, condoned by senior management, deferring payment well beyond the contractually due date, the knowledge that bills will always be paid on time may well make the buyer a highly attractive business partner.
- The prestige that can derive from being known as a supplier to a 'blue chip' organization, especially if that organization is willing to allow the supplier to use the association in its promotional material. Of course if the buyer's company is not a 'blue chip' organization or does not have other public standing we know this aspect will be of limited value.
- The use of simple procurement systems with straightforward uncomplicated contracts. Over-elaborate systems and procedures can make it more expensive and risky for a supplier to trade. In fact one might consider whether highly complicated contracts are really necessary when the relationship is long term with many repeat items being supplied. The prospect of continued business itself may be a more effective regulator than a detailed and possibly complicated contract.
- The perception that there is a genuine opportunity to grow because of the association. Growth could be with an established product or with a new range of products. It could also be an opportunity to break in to a hitherto unreachable market.
- Finally, and maybe most importantly, the perception that the supplier is dealing with a buying organization which is straightforward and open minded and which will not resort to cheap tricks in order to gain a short-term advantage.

All of this not only calls for a reorientation of the buyer's viewpoint, but also will inevitably bring with it an increased workload in those instances in which it is used. Is this extra effort worth while and does it not have its shortcomings and dangers?

ADVANTAGES OF BEING A 'PREFERRED CUSTOMER'

If a buying organization can promote itself as a 'preferred customer' of a supplier, it will achieve advantages not available in the market generally. Among these are the following.

- The ability to buy on an ongoing basis at prices that are highly competitive. Suppliers may well be willing to reduce margins in the knowledge of the advantages that will accrue to them arising from the relationship. These prices may not necessarily equate to very low spot prices which may from time to time be available elsewhere in the market-place.

- The realization of supply-chain economies which may be shared between buyer and seller. This category could include changes in the timing of production, financing of more efficient practices, revised stocking arrangements, and enhanced systems support.
- The provision of a greater security of supply and preferential treatment especially in times of shortage or supply interruption. Both supplier and buyer can work together to eliminate the conditions which have the potential to create supply difficulties.
- Improved quality standards and greater consistency of quality. The use of quality assurance within the total supplier–buyer supply chain will be easier to introduce.
- The ability to develop and quickly introduce innovations in product lines, thus achieving and maintaining a position of market leadership.

DISADVANTAGES OF THE PROCUREMENT MARKETING CONCEPT
The concept is not without its dangers and problems which buying organizations must keep under constant review. Some major concerns include the following.

- The risk of a return to long-term, cosy, and therefore uneconomic relationships in which supplier competitiveness is gradually eroded. This has typically been the problem when purchasing authority and responsibility have been abdicated to client departments.
- Too close an involvement in the supplier's cost structure. If the supplier's costs are logically and fairly built up then it may be seen as logical and fair for the customer to pay the price asked. This is clearly a position which must be avoided in all circumstances.
- Limiting interactions only to preferred suppliers brings with it the danger of losing touch with the marketplace. This might make it impossible to identify long-term adverse trends and opportunities arising from the availability of new and better products and services.
- The temptation to become too dependent on a particular supplier and thus make it very difficult, if not impossible, to change when needed. Conversely, if a supplier comes to rely too heavily on a customer, then that customer starts to assume some kind of moral responsibility for the ongoing health and viability of the supplier.

INVOLVEMENT OF THE PURCHASING FUNCTION

The introduction of the procurement marketing concept into a buying organization will bring with it certain other requirements without which it cannot possibly be a success. Most importantly, the purchasing function will need to be involved in the development of non-purchasing strategies at corporate level.

For example, it may be desirable to promote changes to the traditional annual budget cycle which, in many organizations, determines when goods and services are purchased. A preferred customer may be one who can offer a supplier a longer term and more evenly distributed buying plan.

The purchasing function will also have to have enough authority and prestige to ensure that those conditions necessary to make the company be regarded as a 'favoured customer' can be introduced. Not least among these is the ability to ensure that the accounting function always pay the bills on time.

Some may conclude that this concept seems to ignore the buyer's specific needs—for low price, quality assurance, and prompt delivery of the right quantities. 'If you want to satisfy supplier needs,' they might ask, 'aren't you going to pay more?'

Our answer is 'No'. The organizational goals of the buyer are satisfied by focusing on the needs of the supply-market. For example, a buyer's desire for a low price can be satisfied if the supplier's costs are understood and action is taken to try to lower them. As another example, the long-term needs of the buyer for new products and technical assistance can be realized only if the suppliers find the buying accounts attractive. Conversely, the buyer may be able to help the supplier reduce costs, a benefit which need not necessarily be passed on to all customers.

Reverse marketing

The term **reverse marketing**, to describe the process by which the buyer creates a supply capability, was first coined by Leenders and Blenkhorn in their excellent book of that name (published in 1988).[1] Our purpose here is to give a brief overview of the concept. Readers interested in more detail should read the original text.

The need for reverse marketing arises when the existing supply-market appears to be incapable of delivering requirements in an economic manner. This could occur when there are no suppliers manufacturing the requirements in a convenient location or where the market is distorted by price fixing or some form of allocation. Reverse marketing can also be used where there are overriding social or political reasons for purchasing from a particular location or area.

Reverse marketing involves the buying organization stimulating suppliers to enter a market for the provision of specified goods or services. It can be done by the setting up of a new company, or by persuading an existing company to broaden its range, or by encouraging an existing supplier to expand its area of operation.

One example of the successful application of the concept was the introduction into the UK of a second manufacturer of industrial gases at a time when the market was dominated by one supplier. The customer identified the problem and then encouraged an overseas supplier to establish an operation in the UK, thus providing real competition for the first time.

Reverse marketing is not an activity which can be undertaken by a purchasing function working in isolation. At the outset any initiative must command the wholehearted understanding and commitment of all those affected, including the board of directors. Any attempt by a purchasing function to go it alone will be doomed to failure. In the case of the above example a full strategy was derived, and support obtained from the board of directors before any action was taken.

Reverse marketing should not be applied solely in response to today's needs. It can often be most effective in providing solutions to problems predicted for the future, such as raw-materials shortages or expected environmental restrictions on current manufacturing methods.

According to Leenders and Blenkhorn it is important that the activity is carefully structured to ensure a successful outcome and to avoid wasting time and resource. They propose 11 phases:

- fundamental research
- specific research
- key decision point
- design
- organizational support
- design review
- negotiation
- agreement in principle
- written agreement
- contract administration
- future options.

We shall describe these briefly.

FUNDAMENTAL RESEARCH

Fundamental research examines the current and future positions of all the key supplies and identifies areas where there is a mismatch between the present and future needs (quality, quantity, delivery, price, etc.) of the business and the present and future capabilities of the supply-market. This will highlight specific commodities or services where there would appear to be a discrepancy between needs and availability. This stage would involve the use of supply positioning, supplier preference and vulnerability analysis.

SPECIFIC RESEARCH

Specific research is the foundation of a successful outcome. It takes the options identified in the fundamental research stage and develops them in more detail. This entails developing a true understanding of the nature of the requirement, together with an analysis of all other possibilities including procurement marketing, reverse marketing and AVIP (affirmative vendor improvement programme). All such options should be fully explored prior to taking the decision to move further along the process. It is stressed that reverse marketing should be chosen only if no other realistic possibilities exist.

KEY DECISION POINT

The buying organization will then reach a key decision point where they must decide whether commencing on a major exercise is really needed and whether the effort required will deliver tangible and significant benefits. It is most important at this stage to assess the probability of success or failure.

DESIGN

Having decided that there is a real business opportunity, the buying organization will then enter the design phase. This is really a plan for the development of the project, including a redefinition of objectives, a description of all the steps which have to be undertaken, and the identification of all those including potential suppliers who will need to be involved.

ORGANIZATIONAL SUPPORT

Organizational support is probably the most crucial stage of all. All those involved must recognize that this will be a major undertaking involving radical changes which may affect the way in which their jobs will be performed in the future. It is essential that such changes are clearly identified at this stage and accepted by all interested parties. Without this the organization will run the risk of a huge investment of time and resources to no avail.

DESIGN REVIEW
Design review is really a refinement of the original plan, perhaps taking account of comments and suggestions made during the organizational support phase. It can also enable the design team to dry-run discussions and negotiations with potential suppliers.

NEGOTIATION
The negotiation phase is the point at which the buying organization puts the proposal to the potential supplier(s). Clearly, if a positive response is to be obtained, the buying team must take great care to ensure that the approach strikes a chord with the target supplier. Unlike most situations, buyers will find that this is very much a selling job.

AGREEMENT IN PRINCIPLE
After extended discussion and evaluation it would be hoped that both parties will reach agreement in principle. There will be a realization that the two organizations can work together towards a mutually beneficial outcome.

WRITTEN AGREEMENT
After further review and checking of all the information the parties will then move forward and enter into a written agreement, which will be in the form of a contract, but care should be taken that it reflects the intent of both parties and is even-handed in its detail.

CONTRACT ADMINISTRATION
The contract administration phase is the actual carrying out of the reverse marketing plan and the introduction of the new supply arrangements. This is not the type of arrangement that, once agreed, can be left to operate on its own. It will require constant high-level review and, if necessary, problem solving to ensure that it continues to benefit all parties.

FUTURE OPTIONS
The final phase is concerned with future options. When the new supply arrangement has been successfully running for several years, the buying organization may wish to consider whether the relationship should be continued. An alternative to continuation would be a move to more

conventional buying, having successfully changed the nature of the market. However, due and careful consideration should be given to the value contributed by both parties and the extent to which some form of moral commitment exists.

Where buyers have utilized reverse marketing to change and improve the supply-market, they have achieved very significant payoffs in terms of cost reduction, product innovation, or other competitive advantage.

Affirmative vendor improvement
The systems of supplier appraisal (before the contract) and vendor rating (performance after the contract) are often used by suppliers themselves as a checklist of actions they need to take in order to become the best performing supplier to the customer. Such rating systems are also used as an arm's length tool by which buyers ensure that suppliers reach acceptable standards.

It is becoming increasingly popular for buying organizations to set future performance targets and to inform suppliers that they will either lose—or not be able to obtain—additional business, if they fall below the specified level. Although the goals are appropriate, such hardline approaches may not always achieve them, as certain good suppliers may decide to trade with customers whose criteria more closely match their own philosophy, vision, and culture.

The affirmative vendor improvement programme (AVIP) is designed for the internal use of purchasing departments to bridge an arm's length relationship with the objective of making the supplier feel like a VIP. This programme mainly builds around communications, relationships, trust (if buying and supplying organizations are truly capable of applying it) and understanding each other's needs, strengths, and weaknesses. The AVIP can be described under ten headings:

- select suppliers
- identify communications
- open communications
- understand the supplier's business strategy and objectives
- be more visible
- understand the marketplace
- carry out procurement marketing
- establish a vendor rating system
- implement strategic supplier plans
- provide an incentive for success.

By capturing the hearts, minds, and attention of suppliers, buyers should be able to obtain an effective route towards integrating joint business needs resulting in a more effective supply chain which has less 'noise' in its system. We shall now describe the individual aspects of the affirmative vendor improvement programme.

SELECT SUPPLIERS

Using the supply positioning overview (see Chapter 5), identify the range of relationships needed in each of the four segments and identify the suppliers which fall into each category. This analysis will also help prioritize time and effort or maximize impact.

IDENTIFY COMMUNICATIONS

Further define the above information in the light of current relations and establish a specific plan for each supplier which will also cater for any special requirements you may have with the supplier or the commodity or service in question.

The approach and method of communication all the way through the programme may be phased to bring suppliers from different levels up to the same standard or could be designed to treat the top Pareto or strategic critical suppliers differently.

OPEN COMMUNICATIONS

It is important to establish that there has been a specific step taken by the buying organization in this regard and therefore a conscious start to the programme is needed, even when it is already felt that there are good communications with certain suppliers. It should be remembered that some sellers are trained to make buyers feel comfortable and important and that good relationships exist. The alert buyer needs to consider such flattery and the true state of the relationship before establishing the company's plan of action.

UNDERSTAND THE SUPPLIER'S BUSINESS STRATEGY AND OBJECTIVES

If the buying organization's strategy and objectives do not match those of its suppliers (see Chapter 6), then a long-term future together is unlikely. For example, a supplier's strategy to sell less at higher percentage profit may not match the buying organization's desire to go for market penetration by more competitive pricing methods. Joint understanding in this area can, however, lead to a reappraisal of the situation and agreement either to modify strategies or to find alternative acceptable ways of working together towards separate goals. It has been known for suppliers to walk away from business worth millions of pounds per year because of differently perceived strategies, where a fuller understanding of each other's requirements could have led to a mutually satisfactory agreement for the future.

BE MORE VISIBLE

This is the embodiment of the buying company's commitment to the programme and includes setting up the communication channels, regular information updates, supply conferences, and so on. It may be time-consuming but some companies manage successfully by having quarterly reviews with their suppliers, an exchange of company newspapers, and general accessibility on the telephone.

UNDERSTAND THE MARKETPLACE

Purchasing personnel should have their 'feet in the street' so that they can be sensitive to company and supplier requirements and changes. Loss of business from one customer may lead some suppliers to need more comfort from the continuing existing customers. Change of supplier personnel will require more effort from the buyer to help the new people understand their relationship and business problems and opportunities. This extends beyond the normal sales contacts and stretches through into the supplier organization, for example, new production directors may give priority to customers they know and understand rather than to other customers who are just names on a piece of paper.

CARRY OUT PROCUREMENT MARKETING

This was covered earlier in this chapter and is an integral link in this communication chain. Selling the buying organization as a preferred customer should result in suppliers wanting to listen to the AVIP and then constructively trying to implement it.

ESTABLISH A VENDOR RATING SYSTEM

At first sight, this seems too blunt a device to improve dialogue, especially as it is normally a negative based system, that is, buyers tend to refer to the rating system only when things are bad. However, the old adage of 'what gets measured gets done' aptly applies to the AVIP, in that the vendor rating system will show the suppliers how their improvements are being effective and should provide the opportunity for the buyer to compliment the supplier on achievement as well as discussing any downturns in performance.

IMPLEMENT STRATEGIC SUPPLIER PLANS

There needs to be a framework for improvement so that the buyer and supplier can work together to climb up the ladder of success. These plans are necessarily specific to each supplier but can often be seen as yet another way for the buyer to take advantage of the supplier. The buyer must work hard to offset this somewhat natural opinion. Some customers place a buyer at the supplier's site, especially where large purchases or projects are involved. Such placement brings dividends by greater understanding of each other's requirements and significantly improves communication. Indeed, some suppliers actively encourage sales to professional, innovative, and demanding customers who are therefore used as change catalysts to keep the supplier's organization on its toes. Certain automotive suppliers have done this with Japanese implants in the UK and have quoted extra-competitively to acquire the privilege.

PROVIDE AN INCENTIVE FOR SUCCESS

Profit and turnover may sometimes be lesser motivators than stability, product innovation, or strategic presence in certain marketplace sectors. Consequently, it is important to analyse the supplier's main motivations which will significantly link into business strategies and objectives. The buyer can then relate these to the AVIP and reward the participating suppliers in proportion to the success achieved.

Hence the affirmative vendor improvement programme is designed to make a start towards a more effective supplier base, using the medium of increased communication and the resultant flow of information. Additionally it will force buyers away from the more traditional adversarial relationship towards the balanced partnership–co-makership philosophies which are integral to modern supply chain management concepts.

The Ten(d) to Zero Programme

There are a great number of vendor rating systems in operation. It is important to ensure that any such system encourages suppliers to upgrade their performance rather than being a source of demotivation for them. As an example we now describe one which has had considerable success.

The Ten(d) to Zero Programme is a specific initiative introduced in order to provide a step-change in the performance and effectiveness of the supplier interface in one particular industry. However, the principles on which it is based are easily transferable to other business sectors.

Ten(d) to zero was the name chosen for the programme because it was based upon ten major aspects of the trading relationship and it established a plan to tend the costs of these from the poorest level (10) to the best (0).

Once implemented it created a single rating system for

- supplier appraisal
- vendor rating
- supplier development
- bid comparisons
- supplier integration
- suppliers' measurement of their own performance
- measurement of the buying organization's purchasing performance.

TEN(D) TO ZERO PROGRAMME STAGES

The programme has the following stages:

- Review the buying company's customer requirements.
- Convert these into buying company's needs.
- Convert these into goals/needs from supplying companies.
- Create a 'brochure' to sell these needs.
- Create a step-by-step ladder of improvement towards the goals identified. (This will form the basis of a scoring/rating system.)
- Choose a title for the programme to capture the interest of the buying company and the suppliers.
- Review the concepts with selected suppliers and amend and fine-tune for maximum benefit.
- Establish a 'launch' with the key suppliers involving board members (for strategic commitment) and senior operational personnel (for tactical performance and implementation). This may result in a series of 'launches' to avoid the joint presence of competing suppliers and to provide smaller groups with more individual attention.
- Arrange a series of follow-up meetings (ideally at the suppliers' premises) to go through the programme with them and provide initial scores, showing where they stand on the ladder and highlighting the steps which they have to take to achieve the ultimate requirements. Discuss the scoring and amend as applicable.
- Obtain the suppliers' commitment to the programme and establish time-scales for improvements.
- Coordinate the scores and confidentially publish them within the buying organization. Establish a supply base average (a total and/or by commodity) to provide some initial reference points.

- Establish regular meetings building up to a supplier conference which all key suppliers should attend (perhaps one year after the launch). This provides for a focal point for achievement and provides an opportunity for increased 'selling' of the programme and subsequent motivation improvement.
- Fine-tune/amend the programme to adjust to the learning points of the initial period.
- Continue working with suppliers towards what should now be joint goals.
- It may be necessary to change some of the suppliers, where progress is insufficient or where it is felt that the existing supplier will not achieve or get close enough to the desired goals.

EXAMPLES OF BENCHMARK FACTORS

The factors which are chosen as the benchmarks for the programme will naturally depend on the business and the buying portfolio. There will be considerable differences between industrial sectors. As an example, the following benchmarks were chosen for a situation where the buyer was in the automotive distribution business.

1 Zero transaction cost   This covers the costs of ordering, receiving, and payment. The ultimate is of course electronic data interchange for speed, accuracy, and cost-effective communication.

2 Zero inventory funding   This is designed to remove inventory (and therefore costs) from the entire supply chain, and not only from the buyer. The supplier is encouraged to provide quick response and good availability to improve stock turn.

3 Zero cost penalties   This is an obligation on the suppliers to have competitive prices to meet and beat international competition.

4 Zero warranty cost   This is an obligation on suppliers to give full support for their products with a target of no quibble-warranty.

5 Zero delivery defects   This means accurate physical deliveries backed by accurate paperwork to streamline the receiving process.

6 Zero support costs   This means full support from the suppliers in the form of training and referred orders, to give increased sales to both parties.

7 Zero range gaps   This is full marketplace coverage to maximize sales opportunities.

8 Zero distribution cost penalty (otherwise called *Recognition of the function*)   This is to emulate the more structured US market in ensuring that suppliers' prices recognize the functions performed by the central warehouse and the costs and profit requirement in the distribution chain.

9 Zero obsolescence costs   This is the obligation on the suppliers to support stock and to take back obsolescent stock so that stockholding on selling lines could be maximized.

10 Zero promotion costs   This is the contribution made by suppliers in promotion of the product range and therefore their own products.

EXAMPLE OF SCORING
For each of these factors the buyer will construct specific milestones or targets for the supplier to reach. For example in Factor 1, zero transaction costs, the scoring might be as follows:

Score
10 No commitment to EDI and incomplete/inadequate paperwork.
 9 Manual paperwork systems are reasonable but still have errors.
 8 Manual paperwork systems are satisfactory.
 7 Supplier is committed to EDI and has an acceptable plan to implement.
 6 Hardware and software links are established.
 5 Small number of transactions by EDI.
 4 Approximately half transactions by EDI.
 3 Most transactions by EDI.
 2 All transactions by EDI.
 1 Error-free transactions.
 0 Supplier supports the cost of all transactions.

The steps must be carefully thought through to show suppliers where the priorities lie. For example, when the above programme was implemented, the concept of the supplier funding the development costs of zero transaction costs was purposely left until the end, as it was considered that the benefits to the buying company of EDI would easily offset any implementation costs incurred. In practice, suppliers were keen to implement this sector of the programme as soon as their computer system allowed because they could readily see the financial benefits. For this reason suppliers generally were prepared to bear the cost as they saw it as an investment in their own future.

REVIEWING PROGRESS

On any such programme it is necessary to have a method of monitoring progress and establishing targets and timescales. For each supplier the buyer should agree a series of milestones based on the factors being measured. It should be recognized at the outset that the timescale will be considerable, perhaps running into several years.

Progress against these milestones can then be reviewed quarterly and, as appropriate, new targets set. In this way both buyer and supplier have a record of progress over time and an understanding of the timescale for further achievement.

Experience of implementation of this programme indicates that initially, it will be regarded by suppliers as just another way in which the buying organization is trying to exploit them and drive down costs. It will take time and careful promotion to convince them that the exercise can be mutually beneficial. However, the good news is that where this has been applied, suppliers eventually come to understand that painful though it may be, the programme provides considerable assistance in upgrading their performance and providing them with a competitive edge in the marketplace as a whole.

Summary

The three techniques described in this chapter will, between them, provide buyers with a set of tools by which they can improve their position in relation to the supply-market. Procurement marketing will make potential and existing suppliers more willing to deal with and to provide a competitive edge to a preferred customer. Reverse marketing will create a supply-market capability where one does not currently exist. Affirmative vendor improvement programme will provide a mechanism for significantly enhancing supplier performance.

Notes and references

1 Leenders, M. R. and Blenkhorn, D. L. (1988) *Reverse Marketing*, The Free Press, Maxwell Macmillan, Ontario, Canada.

9

The buyer–supplier interface

The previous chapters have described the supply planning process which is the first stage of any strategic purchasing exercise. Figure 3.2 (reproduced here as Fig. 9.1) showed that the next stage is specific requirements identification.

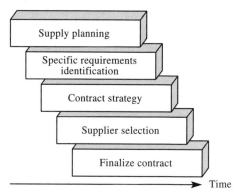

Fig. 9.1 Strategic planning phases

Specific requirements identification

In this specific requirements identification stage, the buyer is commencing to work with the client groups to develop specific contracts to meet firm needs on a defined timescale. The objective of this phase is

> *By working in a multi-functional team, to establish the true nature of the requirement and ensure that the initial interaction with suppliers and the supply-market is managed to produce the optimal result.*

To be really effective, the purchasing considerations and opportunities—

and therefore professional purchasing input—must be taken into account at the earliest stages of this part of the process. This will normally have occurred automatically if there has been a comprehensive supply planning activity.

Early purchasing involvement is very important because there are several fundamental questions to be addressed, the answers to which could have a dramatic bearing on the overall outcome in terms of cost, quality, time to market, etc.

IMPACT OF PURCHASING ON COSTS

The impact of purchasing on costs is illustrated in Fig. 9.2, which relates potential savings to the stage of development of a project. Figure 9.2 clearly shows that the potential at the concept stage is very large indeed and reduces to much more modest levels by the time the production/implementation stage is reached. Claims for savings in excess of 30 per cent are not excessive or exaggerated but it is important to note that they will not be realized solely by slick trading and hard negotiation. Improvements at this level come about from careful evaluation of the true needs of the business thus enabling specifications or indeed requirements to be changed dramatically.

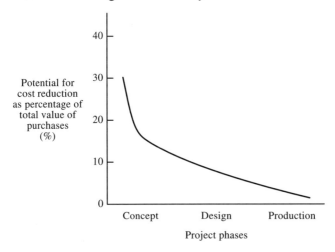

Fig. 9.2 Potential for cost improvement during project phases

EXAMPLE OF COST IMPROVEMENT

A European-based manufacturer used a catalyst in one of its processes which had to be in the form of a very light powder. Investigations had shown that the only source of this requirement was in the USA. Laid-down costs at the user's factory were very high and were making the ultimate product uncompetitive. A cost modelling exercise revealed that the largest part of the laid-down cost was transportation, since the product had to be shipped in containers which occupied a large volume in relation to weight, with consequent freight penalties.

A joint production/purchasing team was set up to investigate. As part of the study they examined the USA manufacturing process with the intention of determining whether they could encourage a manufacturer to set up in Europe (reverse marketing). This proved to be uneconomic due to the large capital requirements and relatively low volumes. However, they identified that the product was made by initially forming a dense cake which was subsequently converted to a light powder using a standard drying process. They were able to change the supply chain so that the product was shipped from the USA as a cake and converted to a light powder at a location near to them, thus reducing volume and transport cost. Taking account of freight savings and changing the drying operation to Europe they were able to save 45 per cent of the laid-down cost.

FACTORS INVOLVED IN COST IMPROVEMENT

It may be helpful to use this example to highlight some of the factors which are required to make this type of exercise successful:

- identification of a significant problem (this item was strategic critical)
- early involvement of purchasing expertise
- multi-functional approach throughout
- full analysis and understanding of the supply chain and its cost elements
- understanding the true needs of the enterprise
- full understanding of the supply-market and suppliers
- cooperation of the manufacturer
- willingness to challenge all assumptions
- willingness to adopt a bold solution.

Above all, the receiving organization needs to ask itself, what it is truly buying. Examples which illustrate this are the following:

- children's nappies: cotton or absorption capacity?
- retail distribution: trucks or delivery capability?
- printed forms: printing or a forms service?
- accounts payable departments: verification and processing service?
- a computer: storage and retrieval service; processing capacity?

In our experience, real cost breakthroughs have come about when multi-functional teams address and get considered answers to these questions.

Getting early involvement

Many buyers claim extreme difficulty in being involved early enough in the purchasing process. They will often claim that by the time they become involved many of the decisions have been taken and commercial options closed out.

Whose fault is this? Those who wait to be invited to participate will wait for ever. Buyers need to become highly proactive if they are ever going to realize their goals.

Here are some of the actions which they can take:

- Review all revenue and capital budgets—identify the areas of large expenditure—and initiate the debate on their purchase, at the same time demonstrating expertise which will add value.
- Regularly visit those in the company who are known to initiate significant third-party expenditures—gain their confidence by talking about their problems and demonstrate opportunities.
- Like all good salespeople, identify the areas of dissatisfaction in their client base and offer opportunities and solutions which will overcome that dissatisfaction. This can be quite important as the incorrect identification can have the opposite effect:

    For example a new purchasing manager found that she was getting nowhere in trying to be involved in buying advertising. The advertising manager was just not interested in offers to cut his costs. Eventually the purchasing manager found out why. The advertising manager had been hired to manage a £10 million budget and didn't want purchasing to reduce it to £9 million which wouldn't look good on his CV. However when the purchasing manager in response offered to provide him with £11 million of advertising for £10 million, she got his attention.

- Again like all good salespeople, if there are no areas of dissatisfaction then create some. This could be more for the money, earlier completion or better quality to name a few.
- Set up an arrangement with senior secretaries that they will give warning when their executives are planning to meet with a supplier—and then send a briefing memorandum.
- Seek invitations to all key planning meetings.

You may not succeed in any or all but it is worth a try and beats sitting around waiting for a requisition.

USE OF THE MODEL

Figure 3.4 illustrated the model for specific requirements identification; it is reproduced as Fig. 9.3.

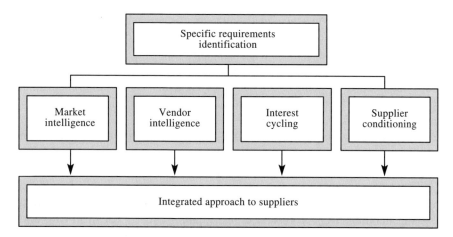

Fig. 9.3 Specific requirements identification

Market and vendor intelligence clearly play a considerable part in assisting the buying organization fully to identify its true needs. No discussion is included here as it can be found in many standard text-books. We would like to devote our discussions to reviewing the time and attention to managing the way in which the staff of the buying organization interface with the staff of the potential supplier.

No amount of supply planning and requirements identification can compensate for lack of thought regarding behaviour when the buyer communicates with the supplier. What happens in these interactions can have a profound effect on the supplier's willingness to respond, and to trade, as well as crucially influencing the eventual commercial outcome. Unfortunately many buyers do not understand the potential for advantage or disadvantage that these interactions present. Some of the underlying features are described in the next section.

Supplier–buyer conditioning

Developing strategies to attract good productive suppliers is obviously very important. However, it is as well to remember that in certain circumstances the supplier's sales organization may be seeking to influence the buyer to ensure that they gain maximum advantage from any particular transaction.

These influences often start very early on in the interactive process by which buyers eventually complete a transaction with a supplier.

For example, in the course of conducting business we often invite buyers to tell us when they think that the negotiation starts. Many will reply that negotiation starts in the first meeting at which contract terms are discussed. In fact, in many cases some negotiation has started well before that, almost certainly at the first contact.

We experienced a situation where, in order to maintain profitability, a supplier needed to achieve a price increase from the existing customers in the region of 20 per cent. Unfortunately for the supplier, inflation was running at 3–5 per cent and the product would have been easily resourceable as there were several other competitive suppliers not subject to the same cost pressures. This appeared to be a seemingly unachievable objective.

The sales organization set up and implemented a detailed plan to reach this 'impossible' target. Over succeeding months the targeted buying departments received telephone calls, requests for meetings, and entertainment proffered during which the cost problems of the supplier were emphasized. Although no price increase was requested, it was made clear that costs had risen by a staggering 35 per cent, mainly due to currency variations.

It was only after this three month period that the supplier sent the customers a written request for a price increase of 24 per cent. Many buyers were relieved that this was considerably less than they had been expecting and very few challenged the figure or tried to negotiate. Out of 300 customers 60 per cent agreed to an increase of 24 per cent or more. Some customers paid the full 35 per cent because, in the course of the previous discussions, some buyers had told the supplier prior to the formal request that they could see that he had no choice but to pass on the increase. Although some customers did object and negotiated lower figures, an average increase of 20 per cent was achieved and only three changed to new suppliers.

Thus the supplier realized the objective of obtaining a price increase well above inflation in a situation where there was competition offering equivalent products at lower prices and without alienating the customers.

In this case the negotiation actually started on the first occasion that the supplier contacted the buyers and informed them about uncontrollable cost increases. By the time the actual request for a price increase was presented, the buyers had come to believe that there was little they could do about it, and indeed in many cases the buyers were very sympathetic to the 'dilemma' of the sales organization.

This illustration is a classic example of what is known as **buyer conditioning**. Good sales staff are trained to condition the behaviour of buyers so that they will react in a predictable way which is favourable to the seller. Most buyers are unaware of this subtle process and certainly few have developed techniques to counteract and reverse it.

Experiments have shown that higher order mammals will react in a predictable manner, when given a lengthy exposure to certain physical and mental stimulae. In many cases the reaction continues even after the original stimulae are no longer present.

The best known experiment occurred in the early twentieth century when Pavlov arranged that every time his dogs were fed, a bell would ring immediately prior to the appearance of the food. In the early stages the dogs started to salivate when food appeared. As the experiment progressed the dogs began to salivate when the bell rang. Eventually Pavlov was able to make the dogs fully salivate by ringing the bell without the appearance of food. By this experiment he demonstrated that it is possible to create behaviour related to artificial stimulae.

'What has all this got to do with buying?' is the cry. Well, as we saw from the previous example, sales staff can use a form of the conditioning process to make buyers behave in desired ways. For example, what is the normal reaction of a buyer when informed by the supplier that there is an imminent price increase? Most buyers fire off an order to get in ahead of the price rise—which of course is exactly what the sales staff want!

Conditioning the buyer

Salespeople have a whole range of conditioning methods, each of which is designed to bring about a specific reaction. It is therefore appropriate to examine some of these techniques in more detail. Among the most common are the following:

- the price list
- discount
- volume purchase agreement and price break
- special deal or special offer
- claiming limited authority
- claiming low profits
- 'you are a small customer'

- differentiating the product
- service and commercial favours
- friendly interest
- entertainment and gifts
- talking to clients and management.

THE PRICE LIST

In Chapter 4 we observed that suppliers will strive to make their asking prices appear to be legitimate, that is have some firm and immovable basis. What better way to achieve this than by issuing a price list? The more glossy and well printed it is, the more it will serve to impress on unsuspecting buyers that the prices being asked cannot be challenged.

All buyers should be prepared to challenge most strongly all price lists when presented to them. Experience has shown that if this is done then very significant price reductions have been realized.

DISCOUNT

It is very common for suppliers to combine the formalized price list with the offer of a 'special discount for a special customer'. This is a powerful conditioning process because buyers are made to believe that they are getting something extra for their company. The discount is designed to make the buyer anxious to buy and reluctant to question the price further.

VOLUME PURCHASE AGREEMENT AND PRICE BREAK

When suppliers want buyers to purchase larger quantities, they resort to the use of volume purchase agreements (VPAs) and price-break mechanisms. Both systems are characterized by some form of arrangement whereby the more that is purchased, the greater the percentage discount. Thus one well-known supplier of computers will offer a discount structure similar to the one shown in the table.

Order value	% discount
Up to £1 million	nil
£1 million to £2 million	3
£2 million to £5 million	7
Above £7 million	8

Apart from encouraging buyers to commit to larger quantities, the techniques also serve to inhibit further discussion on absolute prices.

When the subject is raised by buyers, the discussion is brought round again to the volume discount structure.

If you believe that a ploy such as this has no effect you may be interested in the following experience. A well-known finance organization decided to change its name. It decided to advise all 30 000 investors by a well-presented, personal letter on the new headed paper. Because of price breaks (worth about 10 per cent) that were offered, they decided to purchase 250 000 letters. The remaining 220 000 are still in the stationery warehouse.

SPECIAL DEAL OR SPECIAL OFFER

Suppliers sometimes offer a 'special deal'. Some deals may indeed be special, but more often than not it turns out that they are really no more than routine business dressed up to look like something different.

A key feature of a special deal is that the supplier will often try to give an explanation for it, again with the purpose of making it look legitimate. Thus the salesperson might imply that the company is trying to penetrate the market, that it has surplus stock to dispose of, or that it has obtained very competitively priced supplies. Many times this may be true but it needs further investigation.

An example is double-glazing sales staff who are looking for houses to 'demonstrate their product' and are therefore offering 'special terms'.

CLAIMING LIMITED AUTHORITY

A technique sometimes used to good effect is for salespeople to claim that they have only limited authority. For example, they say that they have no authority to give a discount in excess of 2 per cent. Many buyers will accept this and not take the argument any further because it seems an impossible or at least very time-consuming task. An excellent counter-ploy is to ask who does have the authority and then demand to meet with that person.

CLAIMING LOW PROFITS

As a rebuttal of the buyer's move to seek price reductions, sellers will often claim that they are already supplying at prices close to cost and that their profits are therefore low.

To understand what is meant by 'low profit', buyers should respond with further questioning. As an example, what would be your attitude to a supplier who claims an item is making only 3 per cent profit, and then contrast your attitude to a supplier who says it is making 40 per cent profit.

Would the attitude be different? If yes, remember it might be the same product and the same supplier, who could be making 3 per cent on sales prices, but this might equate to a 40 per cent return on investment.

All claims about profitability should be treated with extreme caution and not accepted without further investigation. However, remember that if you start to investigate and subsequently find that the low profit argument is true, you may have to accept the logic of the argument and the supplier's price.

'YOU ARE A SMALL CUSTOMER'

In Chapter 4 we showed that, in an attempt to resist claims for better treatment, suppliers will often try to discount the importance of the customer to their business.

There are two points to remember. First, small customers can be just as important, and sometimes generate higher profit margins, than larger ones. This is especially becoming apparent to the suppliers themselves as they adopt the key account management concept. Second, if you have 0.5–1 per cent of the supplier's business you will normally be a very large customer indeed. The supplier needs only 100 customers at 1 per cent to provide the entire turnover.

DIFFERENTIATING THE PRODUCT

Good sales staff will spend considerable time and effort in making the buyer believe that the product on offer is quite different (and therefore superior) to all other competitive offerings. You can be sure that they will spend considerable effort on highlighting the special advantages and benefits.

Most professional salespeople take the view that outright criticism of competitors' products can at best be ineffective and at worst, counter-productive. The sales approach is to make subtle comparisons and to imply that while the competitive product is acceptable, the one being offered is superior in many aspects.

SERVICE AND COMMERCIAL FAVOURS

How many times have buyers expressed a sigh of relief when the supplier has got them out of a difficult situation? For example, the supplier delivers an urgent item even though the buyer omitted to place the order on time. It should be stressed that there is nothing wrong with this, and it is what all good suppliers should strive to do.

However, these commercial favours serve another valuable purpose which sometimes make the buyer dependent upon the incumbent supplier. This, in turn, will make the buyer reluctant to change suppliers because 'we may not get the service from the new supplier'.

High levels of service are an essential part of any contractual relationship but be aware that they can cause a buyer to ignore other key areas of the relationship with the supplier.

FRIENDLY INTEREST

All salespeople are taught to learn as much as they can about the buyers. What are their interests, their likes and dislikes? Salespeople keep careful records so that they always appear to remember previous conversations and personal details, such as holidays and families.

Certain buyers are often flattered by this show of interest and as a consequence relax and become more open. The process can also build up a sense of personal commitment to the salesperson, which makes the buyer less eager to find alternative sources.

Buyers need to be aware that this 'interest' is part of a well-trained routine and probably goes no deeper than an attempt to win or retain business. Buyers are recommended to reverse the process by keeping detailed notes on salespeople they see so that they can influence them to offer the most competitive terms.

ENTERTAINMENT AND GIFTS

Modest entertainment, such as a brief lunch occasionally, is regarded as part and parcel of normal business relationships. Buyers should ensure that such entertainment does not happen too frequently and certainly not to the extent that it could be seen to influence decisions. It is also desirable that buyers offer reciprocal hospitality from time to time.

The real problem arises when the entertainment is not modest and cannot be seen as part of a normal day's business interaction. Thus, invitations to Wimbledon, Ascot, or the ballet should be politely declined. Whatever the rationale, they serve only one purpose and that is to influence the buyer.

Gifts are in a similar category. A diary at Christmas or some low value advertising item is perfectly acceptable; more expensive gifts are not, and should be returned immediately. Finally, outright bribes are not as uncommon as some people might believe. Bribes are usually a culmination of gifts and entertainment of ever increasing value in a cycle in which the buyer becomes unwillingly trapped.

TALKING TO CLIENTS AND MANAGEMENT

As a rule, salespeople will seek to get into negotiation with clients and/or line managers. They will have learned by experience that they have a far greater probability of getting valuable information and concessions out of these groups. This is known as 'back door selling'.

Sales staff will then often make reference to these conversations when talking to buying staff, implying that certain agreements have already been made and that the buyer is merely being obstructive.

The key defence to this is to manage the access of salespeople to other members of staff. It would not be in the interest of the buying organization to try to eliminate such interactions as they are the life-blood of product development and improvement. A better approach is to train all interacting staff in basic commercial techniques and to make it clear to them that purchasing should be kept abreast of major interactions with a supplier.

Buyers should be on their guard and on the lookout for the range of conditioning processes used frequently by sellers. However, merely reacting to these initiatives is insufficient: buyers must plan to take control of the interface themselves.

Keeping the seller selling

The principle that should be followed by buyers in interacting with salespeople is to 'keep the seller selling'. All the time salespeople feel that they have got to work hard to make a sale, they are more disposed to grant concessions than when they realize that the sale has been made, albeit without finalizing the terms.

This is best illustrated by reference to the relationship between the buyer's influence and the procurement cycle. Figure 9.4 shows the degree of influence that a buyer potentially has over a seller as the purchase passes through the various phases of the procurement cycle. The Y axis shows relative influence and the X axis represents the procurement cycle, starting with preliminary discussions and finishing with payment.

It may come as a surprise to some that the buyer's influence is relatively low during the initial discussion phase. Many believe that suppliers always respond quickly and positively to an approach from a potential new customer. Our investigations have revealed that this is often not the case, mainly because potential suppliers may not be convinced that there is really any prospect of firm business. Suppliers may feel that they are being used to elicit market and price data so that the buyer has a better basis on which to negotiate with the incumbent

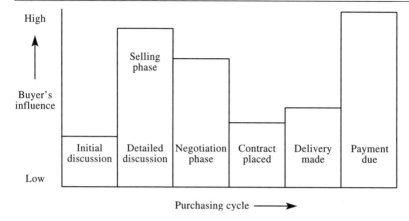

Fig 9.4   Supplier's interest cycle

supplier. They might be aware of various studies which indicate that buyers are reluctant to change suppliers even when confronted with better offers.

INCREASING SUPPLIER INTEREST

It is the job of the buyer to move the process into a phase of more detailed discussions and at the same time raise the level of supplier interest and thus buyer influence. Here is where procurement marketing will play a part. However, there are also a number of remarks that can enhance or depress supplier interest. Those which tend to heighten interest are the following:

- We are undertaking a complete rethink of our purchasing of . . .
- We are aware of your good reputation . . .
- We are seeking to upgrade . . .
- We need to improve aspects of delivery of . . .
- We want to explore new relationships for . . .
- We are interested in a long-term relationship in the area of . . .
- We need your help on . . .

These statements share common characteristics in that they reveal a dissatisfaction with the status quo and therefore an opportunity to change.

DECREASING SUPPLIER INTEREST

Conversely, statements which tend to depress interest are these:

- We thought it was time to check the market for . . .

- We are just checking you out ...
- We have not yet had any discussion with engineering ...
- We are very satisfied with our existing supplier ...
- We intend to split the business ...
- We are asking 15 companies to bid ...
- We are not interested in deviations from the specification ...
- We will evaluate bids on the basis of a written submission ...
- Our payment terms are 90 days ...
- We will impose our terms and conditions ...

These statements tend to show fairly closed minds and a situation where a sale may be difficult. If buyers behave effectively then the discussions will move to the more detailed stage, with the supplier becoming convinced of a real prospect of business. At this time the buyer's influence will considerably increase. This is the 'selling phase' where the sellers are working hard to sell their product or service. They are not yet sure of the business so they are more likely to make concessions, to increase attractiveness, than at any other time in the cycle.

STOPPING SUPPLIERS SELLING

Buyers should make every effort to keep suppliers in the selling phase for as long as possible. Unfortunately many people in the buying organization will have the tendency to stop the sellers selling and move them into the negotiation phase.

Actions which stop sellers selling include indicating to them that they have

- got the deal
- no competition
- by far the best product
- the lowest price
- the best delivery terms.

The following points will also stop sellers selling:

- behaving in a way which communicates any of the above
- behaving in a discourteous or overbearing manner
- having too onerous purchasing terms
- having complicated paperwork or systems requirements
- saying 'Lets talk about prices' (possibly).

When discussions move to the negotiation phase the buyer still retains considerable influence but it will be somewhat less than in the selling phase.

Buyer's influence greatly diminishes following the placement of the order and does not really recover until such time as payment becomes due.

Conditioning the seller

Noting the influence cycle set out above, buyers should plan to take steps to control and influence the sellers. Among the actions to be taken might be:

- concealing certain information
- varying buying methods
- avoiding deadlines
- claiming limited authority.

CONCEALING CERTAIN INFORMATION

Salespeople will always seek to obtain information that will enable them to plan their sales campaign. Buyers should try to conceal certain information if at all possible until the time is right to release it.

In certain circumstances it may be beneficial for buyers not to reveal details of total quantity requirements too early in the negotiation process. This factor can be important in developing a negotiation strategy.

Wherever possible and practical, suppliers should not be advised whether there is competition. However, where it is clear to all that no true competition is available then this stance would lack credibility.

Sellers will often seek to determine the price targets that the buyer has in mind. The buyer should not respond to questions such as 'What is your budget for this item?' as this merely gives the seller an important marker which may be well above the hopeful selling price to sell. Once a marker in the form of a budget has been put down, it is surprising how the salesperson is often able to quote just under that figure.

The final area for concealment is the company's decision-making processes. Good sales staff will invest time and effort in determining how decisions are reached within a customer's organization. They will pose questions such as 'How do budgets get formulated?', 'Who can approve this?' and 'Who sits on the approval committee?' The purpose of such questions is to find out the decision-makers and then plan how best to influence them. There is no reason why buyers should give answers to any of these questions.

VARYING BUYING METHODS

The supplier's conditioning plans work best when the buying organization behaves in a predictable manner and is equally true whether an organization always goes out to competitive bidding, always negotiates, or always undertakes post-tender negotiation. The weakness is always to follow the same procedure. Buyers should strive to vary their buying methods, selecting the one most appropriate to the circumstances. If a variety of methods are used in this way it then becomes much more difficult for suppliers to employ conditioning behaviour.

AVOIDING DEADLINES

Nothing gives a supplier a greater feeling of power than when the buying organization communicates that it is working under some form of deadline. Good negotiators know that the party who is free from a deadline usually has a negotiating advantage.

The first thing to remember is that practically all deadlines are negotiable. It is not uncommon within a buying organization to find that a purchasing deadline has been set by someone in another function who, when challenged, will admit that the reality is somewhat different. The buyer's first task is to determine the true deadline and the degree of flexibility which exists. Even when deadlines exist, these should not be communicated to the seller.

CLAIMING LIMITED AUTHORITY

Just as sellers will claim limited authority in order to discourage attempts to improve the deal, so buyers should consider using the same technique. However, this move has great dangers. If buyers simply say that they do not have certain authorities, they will encourage sellers to ask 'Who does?' and then request to meet with that person. Clearly this would not be in the interest of the buyer.

When communicating a limitation of authority, buyers should try to relate it to the company's management systems in such a way that it is not possible to identify where the true authority lies. For example, a buyer could say that above a certain price, or if other conditions are imposed, it would be necessary to refer to a committee or seek a new mandate from the board.

These conditioning techniques need to be used selectively and with care. Used correctly they can have a dramatic impact on the overall transaction.

Summary

In this chapter we have tried to point out that the management of the buyer–supplier interface needs to be planned carefully and exercised skilfully. Failure to do this can well negate all the good work performed prior to the interface stage.

10

Options for supplier relationships

As the specific requirements identification phase of strategic purchasing gets well under way, the buying organization will need to turn its attention to the development and implementation of a contract strategy, the objective of which is

To define the right contractual arrangements within which suppliers can make a maximum contribution to the buyer's business.

In developing a contract strategy, the buying organization is faced with a tree of decisions. Figure 3.5 illustrated this part of the model; it is reproduced as Fig. 10.1.

Make vs buy

The first decision is whether to perform the work in-house or contract it out. This 'make or buy' decision will be based on a number of perspectives.[1] Among these are:

- Cost analysis
- Power/dependence
- Strategic resource.

COST ANALYSIS PERSPECTIVE

In the cost analysis perspective, the make or buy decision is related to the economic base. Here the organization tries to quantify the financial implications of outsourcing or not. The alternative that affords the lowest cost route is chosen if one looks at cost considerations only. The only real issue here is ensuring that the comparative costs are on an

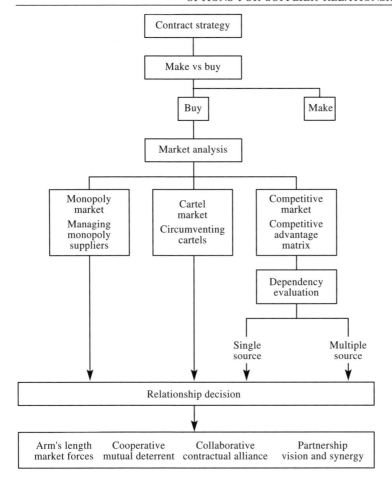

Fig. 10.1 Contract strategy model

equal footing. There is of course plenty of scope to distort the figures to meet the hidden objectives of the proponents.

POWER/DEPENDENCE PERSPECTIVE

It is not possible to restrict the basis for make or buy decisions solely to economic or cost parameters even if they can be accurately and fairly assessed. Such an analysis takes no account of the possible future behaviour of the parties to the arrangement, or how the buying organization sees its role in the marketplace.

A major consideration is whether the buying company can allow itself to become too dependent on any one supplier, either from a commercial or security standpoint. For example, it is not unknown for a supplier to offer a very attractive proposition to a buying organization in order to encourage the latter to disband its in-house capability. Once this has been removed the supplier may be in a position to exploit the situation, especially if there is no other competition. This may not matter if the item under consideration is of low value and little strategic significance, but clearly it is of vital importance if the item is classed as strategic critical.

Buying organizations must therefore weigh up whether a decision to outsource rather than to perform in-house will be in the long term as well as the short-term interest of the organization. Such organizations will have to assess the likely future behaviour of the supplier which may depend on management attitude and the possibility of introducing competition in the future.

STRATEGIC RESOURCE PERSPECTIVE

This is in some ways similar to the power/dependence perspective. It emanates from a division of the company's resources into those that are unique to the company (and therefore are kept and developed within the company) and those that are less central (and can therefore be externalized).

Thus, even though the assessment may be that the risk of exploitation by suppliers will not be significant even in the long term, nevertheless it is felt that the activity is so key to the future of the company that it can never be allowed to pass into the hands and control of others. For example, although a car manufacturer may outsource all of the component parts of a car, it is unlikely ever to do the same with vehicle design. Design is the essence of the organization and the principal factor which differentiates the product. It is quite interesting to evaluate which activities fall into the category of being so core that they should never be outsourced. What would this be for a bank, a transport company, a pharmaceutical manufacturer and so on?

On the other hand an economic assessment may indicate that the organization should start or continue to provide capability in-house whereas the management may not wish to get involved in the organization of activities which at best are peripheral to the main objective. In this case the management may decide to accept additional costs in order to streamline and simplify the business, while at the same time allowing greater focus on core tasks. All of these factors must be taken into account in arriving at the make vs buy decision. The rest of this chapter considers the consequent issues when the decision to buy has been made.

Market analysis

We have shown in other chapters the techniques for assessing and influencing the supply-market. These include supply positioning, supplier preference, and vulnerability analysis. Use of these techniques will enable the buyer to assess whether the market is:

- A monopoly
- A cartel
- Competitive.

For methods and ideas for handling monopolies and cartels, refer to Chapter 12.

Where it is deemed that the market is competitive, the buying organization will be faced with further decisions concerning the best way of operating in that market. For example, should the buyer rely on single sourcing or seek the 'protection' of multiple sourcing? In turn this decision will depend on the relative strength of the buying organization in relation to the supply-market, and certain aspects of the dependency perspective discussed above.

In assessing the relative strengths of buyer and seller we can make use of the 'competitive advantage matrix', discussed later in this chapter.

THE RELATIONSHIP SPECTRUM

Consideration of all aspects of the market and potential relationships will enable the buying organization to reach a decision about the future relationship with a supplier or suppliers. The range of relationships is illustrated in the bottom box of Fig. 10.1. This is not intended to show separated and isolated relationship options but rather that there is likely to be a continuum of relationships with movement to the left or right as experience dictates. This continuum will be described more fully later in this chapter.

It should be stressed that the nature of any supplier relationship cannot always be the sole prerogative of the purchasing function. Many colleagues within other parts of the organization will have opinions, views, and ideas that must be taken into account, especially where purchase items have been classified as strategic critical. This must, therefore, become a multi-functional activity, as indeed are the previous stages.

Supplier relationships: suspicion or synergy?

We shall examine significant trends in the relationship between a business organization and its suppliers. It is no longer appropriate for customers to regard all of their suppliers as subservient adversaries who are automatically expected to comply with the wishes of the all-powerful buyer and to be grateful for the business offered. In fact, this has probably never been the case, despite the macho stance adopted by many buyers. In reality, the buyer is increasingly needing to take the role of 'supplier account manager', motivating the supplier to achieve ever higher performance levels at lower cost. For key supplies, the purchasing focus is moving thus:

In turn, this will have a major effect on the way in which purchasing organizations approach and develop relationships with their supply base. Some organizations are moving away from adversarial, arm's length relationships, to those of closer cooperation and collaboration. For some this trend means a move towards **supply chain management** and **partnerships** and poses a number of important questions. Are these just fashions or necessary trends? Should management of the supply chain be purchasing's prime concern? What is the best way to bind relationships between buyer and seller? Do buyers have the appropriate mind-set to handle these new relationships?

BUYERS' ATTITUDES TO BUYER–SUPPLIER RELATIONSHIPS

Some interesting research has been undertaken in the USA which categorizes buyers' attitudes to buyer–supplier relationships into five types.[2]

1 *Win/win* Respondents in this category exhibit a highly positive attitude towards cooperative arrangements and the mind-set is to develop a long-term relationship that is beneficial to both companies.

2 *Constrained win/win* Respondents in this category also value cooperative buyer–seller relationships but this appears to be driven by needs rather than choice; this would be especially true in a limited supplier or sole source situation.

3 *Realistic win/win* These respondents not only recognize the value of long-term relationships but also seek checks and balances probably

arising from a recognition of the increased vulnerability that buying firms may experience from these types of relationships.

4 *Traditionalist* Respondents believe in managing their suppliers for the purpose of getting what they want. In the end it is the buyer's needs that are paramount.

5 *Holdouts* Respondents are sceptical concerning long-term cooperative arrangements, insisting that suppliers deliver or be deselected and preferring to place their trust in market forces to provide their needs.

In the study, 41 per cent of respondents fell into the traditionalist or holdout categories. The findings are surprising, since respondents were drawn from large aerospace and electronics firms where the move towards cooperative relationships is reported to be quite marked.

Clearly, it will be impossible for a purchasing organization to change its stance with suppliers if all the staff fall into the traditionalist or holdout categories. We experienced this problem when a major purchaser tried to change orientation to the supplier base and was frustrated in the short term by the traditional adversarial beliefs and behaviour of the buying staff.

Before addressing the remainder of the questions posed above it may be helpful to examine those changes and constraints in the supply-market which are causing leading buyers to rethink their position.

Changes in the supply-market
There is no doubt that substantial changes are occurring in the supply-market, some of which are raising questions about its natural competitiveness. Among these are

- rapid technological change
- changing shape of companies
- emergence of new sources
- political dimensions
- rationalization of customer bases.

RAPID TECHNOLOGICAL CHANGE
A dynamic world business environment is responsible for significantly shorter product life cycles. In many cases this requires buyers to acquire supplies of technically complex items from acceptable sources in only a fraction of the time taken in the past and provides less opportunity for the use of cost-reduction techniques such as value engineering.

As a product moves through its life cycle, the customers for it, suppliers' attitudes to it, and its price, all change. Prices and service levels will fluctuate widely unless the buyer moves attention away from individual transactions to look instead at the total relationship between the two companies. It means seeking to understand the supplier company as a living business with its own objectives rather than simply as a source of the product needed.

CHANGING SHAPE OF COMPANIES

The modern commercial environment is dominated by a constant movement in viability and ownership of companies. Many cease trading while others are the subject of acquisitions and mergers on a global basis, thus reducing buyer choice. It often means that the existence of natural competitive forces—which acted between what were once independent supply companies—has to be increasingly questioned as companies become owned by the same holding group. Pricing is not the only concern: there is the possibility of the parent supplier allocating supplies in times of shortage thus introducing further distortion into the marketplace. This trend is especially prevalent for those supply-market sectors which require heavy capital investment to provide manufacturing capability.

EMERGENCE OF NEW SOURCES

As a counterbalance to the above, new sources of supply are emerging as the result of industrial growth and development in the newly industrialized economies of South East Asia and of the political upheavals in eastern Europe. New sources, entrepreneurial and hungry to capture new opportunities, are born when public companies are privatized, or when conglomerates shed businesses that are peripheral to their core activity. In those businesses, such as software development, where large amounts of capital investment are not required, there has been a proliferation of new companies offering a vast range of products.

POLITICAL DIMENSIONS

A major constraint comes in the form of political requirements as they affect purchasing decisions. Some governments, keen to develop indigenous supply capability, require companies to place as much as possible locally. Such practice entails the use of local suppliers who may not yet be world class; this also includes placing of orders through local agents with overseas sources.

Elsewhere, overseas sourcing may be allowed but only to a limited extent, and the government concerned keeps a keen eye on the 'local content' figure which is subject to regular report. Traditionally this had been the stance of the Canadian government and, in some circumstances, the Canadian provinces.

Additionally, there may be legislation requiring companies in some business sectors to provide 'full and fair opportunity' for domestic suppliers to compete for their business. The respective agencies of the UK and Norwegian governments have maintained this posture for purchases relating to North Sea oil development and operation.

EU Procurement Directives have substantial impacts on the purchasing freedom of European government departments and others following their rulings. It is not the intention within this book to discuss either the impact or possible responses to this legislation. However, suffice it to say that those organizations who are required to comply with the directives are having to develop completely new methods of purchasing which will enable them to purchase from the most effective source. They have found that the result need not necessarily be confinement within a set of bureaucratic rules.

Far from releasing a full flow of freely competitive forces which would naturally align high-performing competitive suppliers with 'demanding' buyers, this type of legislation and control introduces artificial and time-consuming rigidities into the system. These restrictions not only are concerned with the 'upstream' processes leading up to order placement, but also include the drain on energy afterwards if there has to be a lengthy defence of decisions taken 'downstream'.

Where formal controls do not exist, corporate strategy may dictate that maximum opportunity be taken to create a favourable public relations image in the placement of key contracts or order.

Whether buyers view these constraints as right or wrong, they do exist and they bring significant intangibles into what would otherwise be a clear-cut analysis of where the order should be placed, on the merits of the best terms on offer.

RATIONALIZATION OF CUSTOMER BASES

As we have seen in Chapter 6, in forward-looking companies the seller's view of business is changing. The trend for strategic sales is to move away from the 'volume-orientated' mentality of the salesperson and towards the key account manager concepts where the focus is on total account profitability; the aim is to ensure a profitable return for all the effort and costs expended in servicing the account.

Consequently, certain supply companies are becoming more selective about who they want to have as long-term customers. Customers not seen as long term will be eased out of the way and—as a first step—will be charged a hefty price increase; this is a nightmare scenario for the buyer who purchases from such a supplier and who is in the strategic critical category of the supply positioning model.

Long-term strategic alliances between buyers and sellers are being set up by some companies as a way of avoiding having repeatedly to engage in re-sourcing activities; for as long as such arrangements hold good, supply capacity, at the margin, will not be available to potential buyers outside an alliance. The choice of alternative sources will effectively be reduced, thus becoming another distortion which moves the supply market a further step away from being 'free'.

The buyer's response to the changing market
So far we have looked at how supply companies are changing their shape and the way in which they look at customers, together with the web of political issues which surround buyer–seller transactions. The result is that the customer companies are becoming more at risk to factors outside their control. A prudent response would be for buyers to develop as wide a supply-market as is possible so as to minimize the risk of being caught out.

What are customer companies doing about the situation? Apparently, they are taking initiatives which are the opposite of what the above trends suggest should be done. Two of the current developments are

- reducing the supplier base
- focusing on core activity.

REDUCING THE SUPPLIER BASE
Part of this comes under the heading of good housekeeping; the rest is a policy to get closer to fewer suppliers. A typical situation is represented by one of the companies with whom we have conducted consulting work. The company has 23 000 suppliers on its approved supplier list of whom only 7500 had been used in the previous two years. Of the company's total annual expenditure, measured in hundreds of millions of pounds, 81 per cent is with only 87 suppliers. (Note that this has not resulted from lazy buying which prolongs cosy relationships with preferred suppliers, but reflects the typical order-distribution profiles found in many organizations.)

The challenge to the purchasing manager is to create conditions in the supply-market whereby buyers can focus their skills on the **strategic few** rather than the **tactical many**. The way forward involves using the supply positioning technique (see Chapter 5), but clearly the road must first be cleared by removing unused suppliers from the vendor list. One result is the considerable saving of effort in maintaining that database. A further reduction in the actual number of suppliers remaining on the list is then often necessary in order to be able to work closely with a chosen few to implement, for example, just-in-time (JIT) arrangements, quality improvement drives, or Ten(d) to Zero Programmes (see Chapter 8).

A cautionary note is needed here. It is worrying to see some companies failing to see the difference between 'vendor rationalization' as a means to an end, rather than an end in itself. The company which sets itself an arbitrary target of achieving a 50 per cent reduction in its vendor base is living dangerously. The objective should be to increase source options for the future and to realize that a phase of working closer with fewer suppliers may be a necessary step along the way (discussed later in this chapter).

FOCUSING ON CORE ACTIVITY

Many organizations are now contracting out work which, hitherto, they did themselves in their quest for high performance and excellent results. The idea is to concentrate effort on what they believe they do best (core activities) and to rely on suppliers to perform functions at which they themselves do not excel (non-core activities). A measure of this reliance is the percentage of company sales income which is spent on purchasing materials and services. Typical manufacturing companies average 55 per cent. Those in high-tech electronics area rise to 70+ per cent. How high can it go? A successful company making heavy construction equipment spends 88 per cent of its sales revenue on supplies. The reason? In the words of their purchasing director: 'every time we launch a new product we buy bigger and bigger assemblies from fewer and fewer suppliers'.

WHAT ARE THE MESSAGES?

First, as concluded by Pilling and Zhang, 'Since long term co-operative relationships often involve both dependence and vulnerability for one or both partners, it is important for firms that are considering this type of relationship to engage in a relatively extensive supplier selection process'.

Second, again arising out of the Pilling and Zhang research, 'Power must be exercised judiciously. The use of coercive power in inter-firm relationships has been shown to weaken their co-operative nature'.

Third, buyers are deliberately restricting their supplier base. The reasons are logical but given the supply-market trends, the risks are enormous unless the purchasing function is organized and empowered to resolve a key dilemma.

The 'dependency dilemma'

The dilemma is that

> *At a time when market trends suggest the wisdom of placing business with many suppliers ... corporate strategy dictates depending more on fewer.*

The dilemma is illustrated in Fig. 10.2.

A	B
Driving force	Driving force
Increasing constraints and distortions in the supply-market	Need to focus output and effectiveness of own company resources to sustain competitive edge
Resulting need	Resulting need
Freedom to have ample numbers of independent genuinely competitive sources to choose from	Closer relationship with fewer suppliers
Why this objective?	Why this objective?
To be able to cover supply difficulties; to get low cost, high value deals; to capture new development opportunities offered by different suppliers	Need to ensure security of supplies from high-performing motivated suppliers who see us as their best customer
How can 'A' and 'B' be enjoyed at the same time?	

Fig. 10.2 The dependency dilemma

The key is to recognize that what appear to be mutually exclusive objectives can be harmonized but that the balance is a dynamic one which has to be actively managed in a forward-looking manner by the purchasing professional.

The dependency dilemma creates a major role for purchasing which is quite distinct from the profit contribution role described elsewhere. In fact, the role reflects the next stage of evolution for purchasing departments once profit contribution is accepted as a 'given' and not needing to be continually proved by monitoring purchasing effectiveness using cost reduction or savings indicators.

Supply-market orientated role for purchasing

We are now in a position to address the questions of supply-chain management, partnerships, and supplier relationships raised under 'Suspicion or synergy?'.

SECURING THE SUPPLY SOURCE ... NOT LINKING THE CHAIN

Some talk of 'managing the supply chain', others of 'supply pipelines'. While it is right to emphasize this aspect of business as worthy of more management attention than hitherto, there is a risk that over-concern with the 'chain' itself takes attention from the **source** it is fixed to, namely, the company's 'stake' in the supply-market. As a result, there is a preoccupation with reducing costs at different stages in the supply chain (e.g. delivery arrangements and inventory management) and with response times and service levels. Although these are undeniably important, and capable of yielding good cost savings and other competitive advantage, they are of little use if the source itself dries up.

Supply chain considerations explain the re-emergence of logistics as a business function in its own right but for the reasons outlined in Chapter 1 we are not convinced that purchasing should be part of it. The points have already been made but bear repetition:

- Logistics is about managing the costs, efficiency, and speed of obtaining goods from supply sources and then subsequently optimizing their movement through production and out to the ultimate customer at an agreed service level to achieve complete satisfaction.
- Purchasing is about securing access to supply sources in the first place (at optimum costs) just as marketing and sales is about securing the customer base to sell to (at optimum price).

The skills and emphasis are by no means the same, calling for techniques and personal attributes that are quite different from each other. The suggestion to place the two functions together, while having some superficial similarity (i.e. both are dealing with the supplier), could result in an inadequate or inappropriate approach to either or both.

However, how a company organizes to execute these functions has lesser importance than the synergy achievable by the unique contributions of the different functions involved and that people of the right calibre obtain the relevant skills and management support necessary to be successful.

We shall therefore explore purchasing's role as one of managing relationships with the supply sources, as distinct from being just another cost component in the supply chain.

THE SPECTRUM OF SUPPLIER RELATIONSHIPS
'Forward in friendship' is a phrase used by one company to capture the spirit in which it wishes to develop supplier relationships in pursuit of improving supplier performance and achieving cost reductions and other competitive-edge benefits. For most companies this may well be in stark contrast to the previously adversarial dealings between buyer and seller. Buyers should therefore realize that in their enthusiasm to follow 'modern fashion', it is easy to make two common and erroneous assumptions:

- *'The day we decide to stop fighting the suppliers is the day we start being in partnership with them.'*
- *'We cannot be friends with everyone so we will have to reduce the number of suppliers with whom we deal.'*

Let us examine each assumption.

The buyer's company has a relationship with all suppliers in the supply-market, or at least with those that know about it, whether or not it buys from them. The company will have an image; it might be targeted as a future sales prospect, or worse as one the seller does not want to have as a customer, based on what the seller has heard about it from others. A reputation as a poor payer is a common reason for this!

From the buyer's side there may be some companies who will 'never' be acceptable as suppliers, perhaps because of their reputation for using unethical sales practices or because their 'core values' as companies are not compatible with the buyer's own. On the one hand, there are companies which insist on offering buyers sales volume incentives in the form of vouchers to be redeemed against travel or gifts, whereas there are companies which offer outright inducements.

In Fig. 10.3 these companies are 'below the line' and will not be considered in any circumstances. Above the line, all suppliers have the potential to supply, subject to their surviving the close scrutiny of supplier appraisal. Supplier appraisal is a well-known technique, covered in many standard textbooks, so we do not intend enlarging upon it here.

	Level	Type	Characteristic	Compatibility
R e l a t i o n s h i p	5	Self-sustaining supplier partnerships (SSSPs)	'Synergy'	Attitude and performance fit
	4	Risk sharing	'Enforcement'	
	3	Operational linkage	'Open and authentic'	
	2	Continued contact	'Competitive games'	Performance fit
	1	Arm's length *Approved suppliers*	'Spot associations'	
		Acceptable suppliers		*Potential* To Supply
		Unacceptable suppliers		No Fit

Fig. 10.3   Supplier relationships spectrum

We now focus on those 'approved' suppliers with whom the company actually does business. Figure 10.3 identifies different relationships between buyer and seller. What is the distinction? It depends on the nature of the purchase, its importance to the buying company, and whether or not the supplier is driven to respond to market forces.

Level 1 is an arm's length relationship. Due to low cost, relative unimportance to the company, etc., it is not necessary to get close, either to the supplier or the marketplace. It is acceptable simply to get a reasonable deal and some competition will ensure that the supplier offers it. 'Convenience, spot purchasing' would typify the relationship.

The desire for operational efficiency (e.g. to avoid repetitive routine purchasing) may well indicate that a continuing association with the supplier would be appropriate but it is important to differentiate between an operational linkage required in this case and a deeper relationship which may be specifically targeted to obtain a competitive edge by working more closely with the supplier.

Level 2 indicates continued contact with a supply-market sector (for example to keep in touch with price trends, etc.) and close awareness of different suppliers' offerings in order to pick on the best when the need to purchase arises. Whether there are continuous or 'spot' dealings with a supplier will depend on what the market forces are motivating them to offer the buyer. The point is that it is the market which is driving the supplier's motivation; the buyer is not having to win it. Significant costs may be involved, so it is worth while for the buyer to play a careful hand. Indeed, 'game-playing' and posturing may characterize the relationship between buying and selling parties but the high level of competitiveness should not be confused with adversarial or aggressive behaviour. In Fig. 10.1 these relationships would be clarified as cooperative.

Level 3 relationships are characterized by open and authentic behaviour. Authenticity means an absence of game-playing or 'manipulative' behaviour. Having chosen the supplier, there is a continuing contact which is focused on achieving a cost-effective and reliable operational link between the companies because the supplies (but not necessarily that particular supplier) are important to the business. However, the buyer does not feel commercially vulnerable because purchase costs are not the first consideration, and alternative suppliers can be found if necessary. Strategic security items from supply positioning would be the subject of such relationships. If the relationship is reflected in a long-term contract, then again this is more for convenience or operational reasons than to capture the supply source. It makes sense for both parties to work together, a sensible relationship based on logic.

At **Level 4**, one of the problems with 'long-term relationships' is the concern that the buyer will lose touch with 'what's competitive' and that both sides thus become complacent. Risk-sharing relationships go some way towards solving this anxiety by scrutinizing and 'approving' the supplier's costings but this leads more often to acrimony than to reassurance.

At **Level 5**, self-sustaining supplier partnerships (SSSPs) allow freedom to look around, simply because it is part of the deal. In commitment terms, SSSPs can be short term, but continuously excellent supplier performance earns a corresponding extension of the commitment.

To those who believe that a long-term commitment is the only way to win a partnership response from suppliers we would say, 'Be careful ... perhaps the seller is conditioning you to think that way'. It is a convenient ploy for filling the order book well ahead.

Another easily made assumption, by followers of fashion, is that 'supplier base reduction' is an important objective to achieve in its own right. With many buyers rightly aiming to improve the performance of key suppliers and to establish close operational links with them, then it helps to focus on a few so as to start making progress. As is said about managing change: 'If you're going to eat an elephant, then do so one bite at a time!'

It is dangerous to stop half-way, having achieved only higher performance from a few suppliers. Supplier reduction programmes must be seen as a step on the road towards a more important goal of having access to high performance from all possible suppliers. This is the only strategy consistent with supply-market trends which, if not recognized, will leave buyers short of choice and open to being exploited by dominant sources.

This scenario may be illustrated as in Fig. 10.4 .

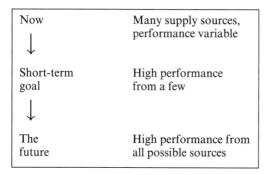

Fig. 10.4   The future (a scenario)

Assessing competitive advantage

In deciding on the most useful contract strategy it will be necessary for buyers to make an early evaluation of their strengths and weaknesses *vis-à-vis* the supply market and similarly whether the potential suppliers are strong or weak themselves.

To assist buyers in making this assessment, the questionnaire set out in Fig. 10.5 lists ten issues relevant to the procurement which determine the balance of power between the buyer and the market (NB not between the buyer and an individual supplier).

Competitive advantage matrix

Procurement considerations		*Weighting*	*Buyer strong*	*Balanced*	*Supplier strong*	
1 Number of suppliers acceptable	High					Low
2 Production or service capacity currently available in the market from suitable suppliers	High					Low
3 Existing share of shortlisted suppliers' current capacity	High					Low
4 Demand growth for product or service required	High					Low/none
5 Substitution possibilities	Exist					None
6 Knowledge of product cost breakdown	Extensive					Poor
7 Knowledge of supplier's pricing policy	Yes					No
8 Supply logistics (e.g. geographical or transportation considerations)	Advantageous					Disadvantageous
9 Attractiveness to relevant suppliers	Strong					Weak
10 Barriers hindering a change of supplier (e.g. cost of change; rigid user requirements)	Insignificant					Significant

Advantageous ————————

Balanced ————————————

Disadvantageous ————————————

The buyer may consider weighing the importance of the ten considerations if deemed appropriate (e.g. if one item is seen to be twice as important as other issues, it would receive two 'ticks' in the appropriate column). However, the buyer must not be drawn into a mechanistic use of the matrix and an unquestioning acceptance of the conclusion.

Fig. 10.5   Assessing competitive advantage

Buyers' strength could be dependent on the percentage of the supplier's business or product sales that they command and on whether their own company plays a dominant role in the market. Strength could also be increased if the buying organization is seen to be an attractive one in the manner described for procurement marketing (see Chapter 8).

The sellers' strength could be dependent on the existence of competition, the availability of alternatives or substitutes, the structure of the supply-market, and whether they enjoy a dominant position for themselves or their product.

Using Fig. 10.5 the buyer can assess the position for each of these other factors and, based on a simple majority, conclude whether the overall position is 'advantageous', 'balanced', or 'disadvantageous'.

IMPLICATIONS OF COMPETITIVE ADVANTAGE ANALYSIS

Figure 10.6 illustrates the purchasing actions/implications which arise from this analysis. It gives a guidance on the preferred purchasing strategies when considering each of price, volume, sourcing, etc.

High ←——————— Buyer's strength relative to market ——————→ Low			
Element of plan	Strength ←——————————————————→ Weakness		
	Advantageous	Balanced	Disadvantageous
Price	Drive a sharp bargain	Drive reductions by optimizing the timing of order placement	Do not emphasize price, concentrate on other aspects of the deal
Contract	Spot/short term; maybe in combination	Combination of spot and medium term	Long term
Volume	Split between suppliers	Induce supplier's interest (e.g. keep supplier unclear about total demand; hide volumes)	Centralize Combine volumes
Sourcing	Possibly multiple	Consider dual	Search for/of develop new supply sources
Inventory	Supplier stock	Consignment stock	Buyer stock

Fig. 10.6 Actions arising from competitive advantage analysis.

Thus, for example, when buyers are in an advantageous position they should be able to drive reductions in price, and look for spot or short-term contracts. They may be able to consider multiple sourcing and negotiate other benefits, such as consignment stocking.

Conversely, when buyers are in a disadvantageous position they must actively seek out alternatives and may have to concentrate on continuity of supply as a priority, rather than price.

Summary

A usual focus for buyers, and especially non-buyers inside the company, is on the product being purchased. The concepts of supply chain management rightly direct attention to the total cost aspect of the supply line, but such internally orientated optimizations are relevant only if the supply sources themselves remain able and motivated to supply.

Trends in the supply-market environment dictate that critical purchasing must focus on relationships with suppliers rather than individual transactions. The concept is to 'secure our stake in the supply-market' and the challenge for purchasing is to create positive supplier attitudes and high performance as might be expected if they were an integral part of our company.

This challenge presents a broad range of issues which demand enlightened responses from purchasing managers and the support of their companies behind them. In particular, it is necessary to be highly selective about the types of relationships which should exist between buying and selling companies, and a model is presented for positioning the relationship consistent with what is expected from it. This objective approach avoids the possibility of supplier relationships being dictated to by fashion, as opposed to the facts of the matter.

Notes and references

1 Brandes, Henrik (1994) 'Strategic changes in purchasing', *European Journal of Supply Management*, Vol. 1, No. 2, June 1994.
2 Pilling, Bruce K. and Li Zhang (1992) 'Co-operative exchange: rewards and risks', *International Journal of Purchasing and Materials Management*, Spring, Vol. 28, No. 2, pp. 2–9.

11

Partnership sourcing

At some stage in developing a contract strategy the buying organization must consider whether advantage can be gained by entering into closer, more cooperative relationships with certain suppliers. In the last eight years such a development has become known as partnership sourcing or partnering. Unfortunately, the term has been used rather loosely to describe a range of relationships (Chapter 10) and regrettably the concept has often been held up as a panacea for overcoming existing problems. Comments such as 'we have a problem with this product or supplier and therefore think we should set up a partnership arrangement' have been put on record.

In this chapter we shall review the practicalities, opportunities, potential, benefits, and dangers of entering into partnerships or strategic alliances, as they are sometimes described. Let us state our position at the outset:

In certain specific instances we believe that buying organizations may obtain significant competitive advantage from entering into closer collaborative relationships with selected suppliers of key commodities and services. However, such arrangements should be undertaken only after careful and detailed evaluation and should be conducted only with those suppliers who can demonstrate integrity and commitment of a high order.

This chapter will be devoted to developing our hypothesis.

What is partnership sourcing?

Partnership sourcing is a commitment between a customer and a supplier to a longer-term relationship based on trust and clear, mutually agreed objectives. The sharing of both risks and rewards of the partners' joint activities is fundamental to the concept; as are their common goals of world-class capability and competitiveness, the elimination of waste, acceleration of innovation, and expansion of the market.

Every word in this definition has been carefully chosen to help give clarity of understanding to the meaning of the concept.

- **Commitment** means that there is a contractual bond between the parties.
- **Longer-term relationship** means that both are planning for the future but not necessarily for ever.
- **Trust** includes openness, honesty, and integrity.
- **Mutually agreed objectives** implies that both parties have sat down and worked together to agree precisely the objectives that they would like to strive for and that their individual goals are compatible.
- It is difficult to conceive of a true partnership where both parties are not **sharing in both risks and rewards**; this is the essence of the arrangement and without this it would tend to become nothing more than a long-term contract.
- **World-class** means that each customer or supplier must measure its business standards against the best in the world. In today's increasingly global marketplace, measuring performance against what is available in a single country is no longer appropriate.
- **Capability and competitiveness** is crucial to the arrangement. Both parties have identified the need to work together to make their respective businesses as keenly competitive as possible.
- **Waste** includes cost reduction but in addition looks at all other aspects of business where resources are used inefficiently.
- **Innovation and expansion of the market** are included to provide a wider vision of the relationship.

Overall it must be stressed that partnership sourcing is not an end in itself but rather a means to an end. It does not replace other good management practices but complements them. It is but one option among several to be considered at the contract strategy stage of strategic purchasing.

Why develop partnership sourcing?

Partnership sourcing is not normally developed or implemented by customers and suppliers as an esoteric and theoretical exercise. The purpose of entering into such an arrangement is for both sides to obtain tangible and visible benefits. These should be agreed and built into the original mutual objectives which are defined at the beginning of the new relationship. From the customer's point of view the benefits being sought will depend in turn upon its strategic posture.

Alternative postures for a manufacturing organization might include overall cost leadership, product differentiation, or market segment focusing. Cost leadership (CL) allows the company to position itself as the lowest cost producer in its industry. Product differentiation (PD) allows it to offer unique products or services. Market segment focusing (MSF) allows the company to cope with competitive forces by serving only a narrow market segment.

There are six typical benefits that a partnership sourcing relationship should bring to the customer.

- Reduction of lead times and increased flexibility in response to company needs and ultimate customer requirements (PD, MSF).
- Reduction of stock and administration costs and improved cashflow (CL).
- Improved long-term planning of volume requirements through availability of higher quality data (CL).
- Innovation and technological advancement through better demand, technical input and design information flow between customers and suppliers making full use of the technical resources of both parties (PD, MSF)
- Reduction and elimination of shortages in key goods.
- The ability to bring new products to market or to complete major projects in shorter times than any competitor (PD, MSF).

Declared partnership goals

Some research in the USA—as shown in Fig. 11.1—puts a rather different light on buyers' goals in this respect.[1] The data are extracted from answers to a questionnaire and show the percentage of respondents who listed particular goals as a reason for entering into a partnership arrangement.

Reduced inventory	76%
Cost control	75%
Dependable supply	70%
Reduced lead time	67%
Reduced paperwork	46%
Improved quality control	43%
Technical support	23%

Fig. 11.1   Declared partnerships goals

It is interesting to note that the most common responses are self-orientated and relate to what might be described as the more mundane aspects of the purchasing challenge. After all, inventory, cost, supply security, lead time, and quality are the most basic objectives of any good purchasing professional. Reduced paperwork is laudable and can yield substantial costs savings but these are minimal when set against the broader purchasing objectives mentioned earlier in this book. There is little evidence of opportunity for shared risk and reward.

In contrast, note that only 23 per cent sought technical support and apparently none—or too few for the sample—gave prominence to innovation, design excellence, time to market, or market expansion; yet it is in these areas where one would expect to see full customer–supplier partnerships yielding benefits which could transform the competitive position of both parties.

Indeed, these are the very aspects in which certain sections of Japanese manufacturing industry (notably motor cars) have been so successful. In the case of the car industry, the manufacturers tie in their first-level suppliers at the earliest stages of design and development, thus ensuring full involvement in design and construction studies. Such parallel engineering enables Japanese manufacturers to develop and bring products to market much more quickly than their western counterparts and also to achieve a significantly lower level of quality defects.

DRAGGING IN ADDITIONAL VALUE
In our view the greatest opportunity for the development of a partnership relationship arises when both parties work together to 'drag in additional value' to the relationship. This concept requires further explanation.

If a buyer and seller focus entirely on price in the setting up of a contract, they will be engaged in a **zero sum game**, demanding wealth rather than creating it. A movement in price benefits one party at the expense of the other and the exercise becomes a trade-off, hopefully with some overlap between the seller's lowest expectation and the buyer's highest. We call this the **price tunnel**.

Of course, most transactions tend to take account of a number of factors or variables, such as payment terms, warranties, etc. (for an extended list see Chapter 12). Each party has to trade these with the other, hoping to give something which costs little in exchange for an element of high value. Quite often deals can be improved for both parties by careful trade-off of such variables which results in what many people term the 'win/win negotiation'. We call this the **contract box**.

Working within the contract box can result in considerable improvements but this depends upon each party having variables to trade and receive. Thus, payment terms can be a tradable variable only if the value in monetary terms is different for each party. This may be in the final analysis, because one party is borrowing at high interest rates and the other has funds on deposit on lower rates.

As has been stated, true partnerships can be created and survive only when it is possible to add value. As a start let us look at an example from the construction industry, not normally noted for close collaboration between parties.

AN EXAMPLE OF PARTNERSHIP SOURCING

A major retailer with some 400 outlets undertook a market survey and concluded that it was necessary to upgrade all of its outlets over a four year period. The upgrading was extensive and so it was decided that in each case the facility would be knocked down and rebuilt from ground up. At that time the industry average for a project of this nature cost £400 000 and an elapsed time of 180 days from shutdown to restart. Construction activity was low and it was a buyer's market.

In this situation, conventional wisdom would be to exploit the market and drive prices down by competitive bidding. Indeed, this would be the conclusion arising from any supply positioning analysis classifying the projects as tactical profit. By use of competitive bidding and subsequently applying post-tender negotiation rigorously it should be possible to get very good prices, particularly if eager contractors were to be offered a contract for several sites at any one time. The retailer's management estimated that it would be possible to reduce the average price to £360 000 but without improvement in construction time.

In the event, the retailer decided to take a different approach. Careful evaluation of the supply-market identified a contractor who appeared to have a high level of capability and whose management exhibited considerable commitment and integrity. After extensive discussions the retailer placed a contract for all 400 sites on the basis of increasing improvement in cost and shutdown time. Both parties agreed to cooperate closely to find new methods of working which would reduce cost, lessen shutdown time, and increase profit for the contractor.

The fifth site was completed for a cost of £380 000 and in 170 days, a somewhat modest achievement. However, improvements continued with each site, as both parties progressed on a learning curve and the fiftieth site was completed for a cost of £375 000 and in 30—yes, 30—days. Although the costs of the rebuild were not dramatically improved, the retailer started to obtain an additional 150 days' trading on each site. This substantially improved profit and cashflow for the retailer and enabled the contractor to considerably enhance profits.

The improvements came about because both parties operated on the basis of trust and cooperation. With the knowledge that it would not be necessary to compete for the remainder of the sites, provided there was continuous improvement, the contractor set about finding ways of building at lower cost and in shorter time, by investing in facilities and equipment which increased offsite fabrication and reduced onsite construction time. Both parties worked together to find design modifications which would aid this process.

Thus, the two parties were able to move outside of the price tunnel and the contract box, and to find ways of 'dragging in additional value', in this case epitomized by the extra trading days. In other circumstances this additional value could have been achieved through design excellence which would have contributed to expanding the market and sales, or for providing a major breakthrough in costs.

The compelling reason for undertaking partnership sourcing is to gain a competitive advantage for the buying organization. It is not the automatic route and it should be undertaken only after extremely careful evaluation of all of the alternatives.

Key issues

Before proceeding to examine some of the more practical aspects of partnership sourcing it may be beneficial to examine some of the key issues which surround the concept, some of which are not always addressed in the depth they merit.

First, there is the risk of being exploited if one party adopts open collaborative behaviour while the other continues to operate in a manipulative way even while professing something different. Second, even when both parties want to change the relationship, the underlying psychology and influences outside it can considerably alter the outcome and inhibit a good result. The next two sections will, in turn, examine the underlying psychology and the outside influences.

THE NATURE OF PARTNERSHIPS

The history of most commercial transactions is one of adversarial relationships between buyer and seller. Many see it as a competitive game in which the winner takes all and this is reflected in some of the 'conditioning methods' described in Chapter 9. It is a tall order indeed to expect all parties to now adopt completely opposite forms of behaviour and to cooperate.

It is often said that people, not companies, do deals. While this is not entirely true, as will be seen later, there is no doubt that personal factors play a large part in the nature of transactions between companies. At this point it may be an opportune moment to refer to some of the research that has been undertaken on the nature of partnerships between individuals, and then to extrapolate this thinking into the commercial arena.

It is interesting to note some of the conclusions which arose from the social exchange theories developed by a number of researchers, who took as their central theme the premise 'that individuals will always seek to maximize their outcomes in any relationship'. If this is true of individuals who play by far the largest part in any commercial transaction, then it will almost certainly be true in commerce. The principal conclusions and their implications for commerce are as follows.

- On a one-to-one basis, relationships build slowly and in a systematic fashion with progressive levels of trust and intimacy. This would suggest that it would be wrong for any organization to seek partnerships with organizations hitherto unknown to them. A partnership relationship should evolve out of previous good experience with suppliers that are familiar.
- Mutual self-disclosure builds trust. On a personal basis, it is difficult to trust someone who you believe is holding back. Only when a person makes revelations to another, thus making themselves potentially vulnerable, can the relationship progress beyond the niceties of day-to-day interchange. While it is common for buyers to demand an 'open book' from suppliers, the reverse is hardly ever considered. Yet, for a partnership to exist, the buyer may eventually have to be prepared to reveal a substantial amount of information about the plans and economics of the business, even if this makes the buying organization potentially vulnerable.

- Individuals expect reward for effort put into a relationship. In the same way, suppliers will expect to see an adequate return for performing in a different way. A partnership will not flourish unless both parties can realize improved profitability. There must also be a perception of fairness, both in terms of effort and reward.
- Individuals remain in a relationship only if outcomes are above a minimum level. Again, this implies that there will be a minimum level of supplier performance which is acceptable. This is not really any different from the normal buyer–supplier relationship.
- People assess their relationships in the light of the benefits, cost, or profit that such associations might bring them. This appears to imply that even on a personal scale, individuals are constantly reassessing their relationships with others and comparing the 'benefits' with those that might be obtained by terminating them and creating alternatives. So it is in commerce and it remains the most difficult obstacle to stable buyer–seller relationships, which can be further exacerbated if those involved in the purchasing process feel they are required to demonstrate to others in the organization that they are getting the best deal.

Partnership sourcing will work only when both parties feel that they are not being exploited. They must feel secure that the relationship is on a sound footing and that it will continue for the foreseeable future. Both parties must be able to discuss problems frankly and constructively; a disagreement does not signify the end of a relationship, rather the beginning of its improvement.

Pilling and Zhang have shown that

> *There is no guarantee that exchange partners can successfully manage these types of relationships to produce mutual competitive advantage. The primary reason for this threat is that the dimensions that characterise close working relationships also provide both increased opportunity and incentive for opportunistic behaviour. In this context, the most relevant dimension is the irreplaceability of the exchange partner.*

(Pilling and Zhang 1992)[2]

OUTSIDE INFLUENCES

We referred earlier to the concept that it is people, rather than organizations, who do deals. While this is true for the greater part, it does need to be recognized that all of us are, to a greater or lesser degree, influenced and shaped by our environment. This must hold good for both buyer and seller, as behaviour of the individual is modified, to some extent, by their respective organizations.

BUYER–SUPPLIER RELATIONSHIP INTERDEPENDENCIES

In our view, for two commercial entities to work together purposefully they will necessarily be influenced by four interdependencies:

- a minimum level of compatibility between the supplying and purchasing organizations
- the level of influence exercised by the purchasing organization on the person interfacing with the supplier, through both official and unofficial channels.
- the level of influence exercised by the selling organization on the person interfacing with the purchaser, again formally, or through unofficial channels
- the relationship between the two interfacing people.

All four interdependencies need to be in balance for commercial partnerships to succeed, as shown in Fig. 11.2. The figure shows that there is an area where all four interdependencies overlap, signifying congruency of objectives and style.

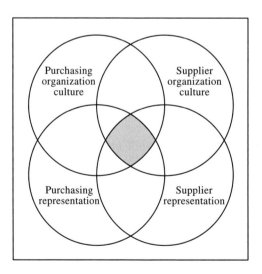

Fig. 11.2 Buyer–supplier relationship interdependencies

Breakdown in personal interface

If the interdependencies are not in balance, or if there is any disturbance of them, this could result in a situation where compatibility is reduced and the partnership would collapse. What is probably the most important interaction is that between the interfacing people. A particular relationship will probably have been built up slowly over time and comprise the need for some personal satisfaction, some logic, some self-disclosure, a range of vested interests, and a mixture of authenticity and manipulation. Trust, if it exists, will have built slowly but could be lost in a trice. All of the factors described in the previous section will be present. What then happens when a company decides to change the buyer or the seller? If this change is not managed effectively then the situation shown in Fig. 11.3 could arise.

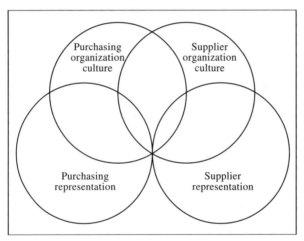

Fig. 11.3 Breakdown in personal interface

Here, such personal relationship as has been built up carefully over a period of time is destroyed. When one party is replaced the other will immediately be overcome by doubts about the future, including whether the new incumbent—for personal reasons—will exploit any vulnerability. There is, therefore, a real danger that a breakdown will occur unless both organizations make provision for such a change in setting up the relationship in the first place. Personnel change must therefore be considered an important part of the setting up of a partnership.

Organizational non-congruence

The problem described above will be ameliorated to some extent if both organizations have a common set of goals and objectives. However, it is possible that the organizations themselves could drift apart as shown in Fig. 11.4.

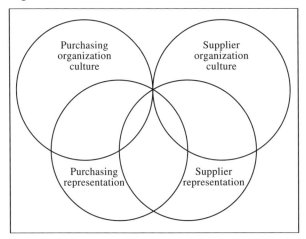

Fig. 11.4 Organizational non-congruence

This could happen on account of a take-over or a policy change arising in itself from a management change. It is in this situation that those at the personal interface will be unable to run an effective partnership, no matter how great their individual commitment.

Individual and organizational non-congruence

Finally, there is always the possibility that one or more of the individuals will themselves become out of touch with their organizations, as shown in Fig. 11.5.

This will be a very real possibility if these partnership sourcing concepts are developed solely within a purchasing or sales organization and with no true understanding or commitment from other key areas within the host organizations. This is why we stress that any move to partnership sourcing must have multi-functional and senior management support.

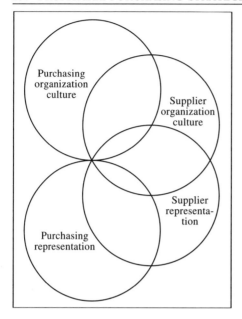

Fig. 11.5 Individual and organizational non-congruence

Differences in western and Japanese practices

In the western world the buyer–supplier relationship has traditionally been adversarial and it would be a mistake to believe that the mere expression of good intentions would be sufficient to change it. In addition, companies in the west function in economic climates where they are expected by the banks and the stockmarket to produce good profits in the short term, whereas these more cooperative relationships are essentially long term in character; it is especially true of suppliers who look to large, short-term margins to sustain profitability and hence share price.

This is in distinct contrast to other commercial climates, notably Japan, where the institutions tend to work more closely with industry, sharing goals that have a horizon of ten years or more. This is surely an important reason to be cautious of attempts to translate Japanese practice uncritically on a wider scale into western Europe. Indeed, there is already a body of evidence that suggests that these 'partnership'-type relationships are proving hard to sustain outside of Japan and, more recently, even inside Japan, where recession is adversely affecting the performance of the economy.

This is not to suggest that such relationships cannot be profitably developed and maintained in Europe but rather to indicate the need for extreme selectivity and care and attention in planning a joint approach, given the fullest commitment from both parties to sustain them.

SELECTING A PARTNER

An essential aspect of partnership sourcing is the method employed by the buyer in selecting a partner. The prime importance of selection of the appropriate partners will remain absolutely crucial to the process as that supplier will gain from the buyer considerable commercial information which could be exploited if the supplier is disposed to do so. Furthermore, changing suppliers who attempt to exploit relationships will become more difficult as the learning curve develops.

Whatever the methodology, is there a way of selecting the right supplier? Many companies are still using **competitive bidding**. Support for the argument for adopting this procedure relies upon the explanation that in this way it is possible to start with the most competitive supplier and then apply development techniques, although it rather begs the question as to whether that supplier wishes to be developed in this way, or indeed has the inherent capability to respond to the buyer's initiatives.

Competitive bidding is an adversarial buying practice designed to enable buyers to operate in an unfamiliar market. It can even satisfy the auditors. However, it is a poor vehicle for selecting a supplier with whom the buying organization may be doing business for an extended period. It does not allow comprehensive evaluation of all the factors which fashion a good partner.

Characteristics of a good partner

Good partners should have the following:

- management mind-set for change and improvement
- absolute honesty and integrity
- willingness to take a long term-view with respect to profit and income
- willingness to share risks
- determination to invest in research and development
- willingness to share information and intellectual property rights (IPR).[3]

It is more likely that correct appraisal of these factors will emerge after some experience of dealing with a particular supplier. There will be a track record of high performance and reliability.

OTHER ISSUES

One issue relates to the time that such a relationship will last. Some buyers think that it is necessary to have a never ending contract. In our view the relationship should continue for the period of the natural life of a project. Duration could be measured in years but it could also be much shorter. Obviously, supplier comfort is indexed to the more continuity that the buyer can offer. More importantly, absolute honesty is an essential ingredient at the outset when defining the duration.

Another issue arises from the common assumption that partnerships imply single sourcing. While this may well be an inevitable result in many cases, it need not necessarily be an absolute rule. Again, it is important to be absolutely honest and straightforward at the outset.

Recognition consequentially emerges, after studying the key issues, that the first step along the way to partnership sourcing is that there has to be an attitude change in management. In turn, this implies longer-term thinking and practices. Most of the balance of this chapter is structured to help management think through both the changes in behaviour and the practices which need to be implemented in order for partnership sourcing to function properly.

Partnership sourcing in action

ESSENTIAL INGREDIENTS

The following points are considered to be the essential ingredients for successful partnership sourcing.

- Genuine commitment from the top of both organizations to make it work. Ideally, a target arrangement should have been discussed at the highest level before negotiations progress too far. The importance of this factor cannot be overstressed.
- A definite understanding by both parties of what is expected in principle and in detail. In both parties, it calls for capable people to be sufficiently trained to carry out their jobs effectively.
- Sufficient resources to ensure success. It is unlikely that any one buyer would be able to cope with more than three active partnerships at any one time.
- Patience to tackle obstacles and teething problems. It will not be a straightforward process; there will be problems and misunderstandings and reactive responses will not be an effective substitute for careful evaluation on a joint basis.

- Open communication between both parties, at all levels and across all functions.
- Action, as well as words, including a preparedness to undertake more than is contracted on paper.
- Trust, and what is meant here is goodwill trust. Mari Sako defines **goodwill trust** as keeping an open commitment, with a willingness to do more than is formally required, and being prepared to accede to a request from the partner or to any observed opportunity that would improve performance.[4] Implicit in this is that partners refrain from opportunistic behaviour.

WHERE TO START?

To start partnership sourcing, considerable emphasis needs to be placed upon preparation, analysis, and planning, internally within the buying organization. A prolonged period of dialogue may well be required to establish the principles and the framework of how to go forward.

As mentioned previously, it is essential to begin at the top. Senior management at the highest level must buy-in totally to partnership sourcing, as a concept, even if they do not fully understand at the beginning what this means in practice. As partnership sourcing is not appropriate for every single customer–supplier relationship, some kind of selection process needs to be undertaken to determine a shortlist with whom to start. Those items which supply positioning defines as strategic critical are the place to start.

Specific internal steps

- Publicize to management within the company what partnership sourcing means and implies. The key is to get commitment from senior management.
- Decide with whom it is appropriate to create a partnership as it will not be valid for every single purchase (supply positioning). Start with strategic suppliers.
- Set clear, simple and easily achievable targets.
- Create a mechanism for driving partnership sourcing forward.

External action

Once the internal decision-making and preparation have been completed, attention should be turned externally to the supplier. The aim should be to create appropriate mechanisms to go from the planning stage through the selection stage into open publicity and open dialogue. External action would include the following:

- Improve the detail and quality of information on suppliers.
- Select those potential supplier partners with care, making full use of the supplier preference analysis.
- Publicize partnership sourcing to the suppliers, e.g. open day or briefings.

Once an organization starts to publicize the partnership sourcing initiative to suppliers, the consequent process will take time and effort and many different questions will be raised. These will have to be answered if the process of building understanding with suppliers is to be successful.

SOLVING PROBLEMS

Though the case for partnership sourcing is persuasive, getting there will not be easy. There will be numerous obstacles and difficulties, particularly early on, as both buyer and supplier are at the beginning of the learning curve. In many ways it is through the solving of the problems that the customer and supplier relationship and bond becomes strong and more effective.

There are eight typical problem areas that customers and suppliers who are interactive in partnership sourcing tend to face during the process.

1 *Impatience* Partnership sourcing takes time to develop properly—often years, not weeks.
2 *Arrogance* The ability to acknowledge that the purchaser's own internal systems and procedures need improving, and that their partners may be able to teach them, must be learned.
3 *Complacency* Continuous measurement and assessment of performance is crucial for both parties.
4 *Willing but unable* Many suppliers would be eager to enter partnership relationships if they felt more confident about dealing with buyers from large organizations. The buyer must be prepared to adopt problem-solving techniques openly, rather than be adversarial.
5 *Able but unwilling* Many suppliers may see no incentive to improve current commercial relationships. If, despite repeated attempts to persuade them otherwise, a supplier persists in being unwilling or arrogant, choose another partner.
6 *Separation* Occasionally a supplier will wish to pull out despite a

successful long-term relationship. Both parties should work profession-ally to make the separation mutually painless; it is essential to design a way out when setting up a partnership.

7 *Over-dependency* For the buying company, partnership sourcing means fewer suppliers; for the supplier, bigger orders. Openness and dependency are implied in partnership sourcing.

8 *Already engaged* Buyers may find that their prospective partner is already in a relationship with a major competitor. In one sense that is good, they will already know how to go about successful partnership. On the other, the buyer may have problems of confidentiality of informa-tion.

MEASUREMENT

In order to measure progress both the measurement system, and then clear simply defined targets, must be present at the beginning. The area of measurement does sometimes get neglected during the establishment phase because it has as much to do with process of change as it has to do with achieving tangible, quantifiable targets in terms of technology improvement or cost reduction, or service.

Targets are essential to both parties to keep the exercise on course, to gauge success and to provide incentives, but they should not be over-optimistic and they should be regularly reviewed to avoid complacency.

Summary

The cultural challenge of partnership is immense. The traditional skills of buyers and sellers, their personalities, training and status, may not yet be sufficiently developed either to practise partnership or to influence the shapers of opinion within their own and their suppliers' organizations. Changing values and success criteria require champions with influencing skills which are quite different from those developed in confrontational win–lose relationships.

Notes and references

1 Presutti, W. D. (1992) 'The single source issue: US and Japanese sourcing strategies', *International Journal of Purchasing and Materials Management*, Vol. 29, No. 1, Winter.

2 Pilling, Bruce K. and Li Zhang (1992) 'Co-operative exchange rewards and risks', *International Journal of Purchasing and Materials Management*, Spring, Vol. 28, No. 2, pp. 2–9.

3 This is very much supported by R. Landeros and R. M. Monczka, who say 'In a co-operative buyer seller relationship, information must be exchanged to develop a credible commitment between buying and selling firms'. Landeros, R.

and R. M. Monczka (1989), 'Co-operative buyer/seller relationships and a firm's competitive posture', *International Journal of Purchasing and Materials Management*, Vol. 25, No. 3, Autumn.

4 Sako, M. (1992) *Prices, quality and trust: inter-firm relations in Britain and Japan*, Cambridge University Press.

12

Monopolies and cartels

An apparently competitive supply-market will be distorted if monopolies and cartels are in operation. Such predatory influences cannot be taken lightly considering the elemental factors to be taken into account when planning a successful contract strategy. Such distortions can render many otherwise effective purchasing practices quite useless, with a resulting loss of competitive edge to the buying organization.

Buyers can operate only with extreme difficulty under these market conditions and such aberrations pose a daunting challenge to the purchasing function. We are frequently told that

> *Your buying theories are all very well but they do not apply as we have to deal with just one supplier.*

Or

> *The suppliers have tied up the market and we cannot do anything about it.*

Both of these situations are difficult—but not impossible—to manage and the outcome is by no means predetermined. In fact, one of the real distinctions between the highly skilled and well-trained professional buyers, and the remainder, is the way in which they approach and handle market distortions.

In both cases, buyers must be prepared to act in an innovative and perhaps unpredictable way, not necessarily conforming to the rules which the buying organization may wish to apply to the major part of the purchasing operation. The nature of these distortions, the conditions that create them, and what can be done to reduce their impact on the buying organization, will be examined in this chapter.

Monopolies

A monopoly exists where the choice of supplier is effectively limited to one.

REASONS FOR MONOPOLIES

A supply monopoly may arise for a number of reasons:

- The supplier may enjoy a genuine monopoly in providing a product or service, due to it being unique, with no challenge from an acceptable substitute. The product may be new or the supplier may be in a strong position to enforce patent rights and so prevent alternatives being manufactured or offered.
- The designers or the end-users, be they external or internal, may specify precisely the particular components or services to be used, or the source from which they must be obtained. Often, such preference is expressed by reference to brand names or the nomination of pre-selected companies.
- Government policy or other considerations of a political nature may indicate that purchasing from certain sources would be 'undesirable' thereby excluding alternatives to the 'approved' supplier.
- The buying company may have other units within the corporate framework capable of supplying the necessary goods or services in conformity with any internal directive, implying preferential use of the in-house sister company.
- The buyer may be locked into a situation whereby it may be totally uneconomic to re-source, for example using alternatives for particular types of machine spares or computer systems might mean major changes or lead to problems over compatibility.
- Possible alternative suppliers may well exist elsewhere, but at such a distance that transportation costs make this proposition uneconomic. However, as can be seen later, buyers should not automatically eliminate them solely for this reason.

Determining the extent of a supply-monopoly

When faced with the kinds of situations just described, there may well be a feeling that the buyer can do little or nothing and that the only course of action is to pay the price and accept the terms asked. It must be emphasized that ideal solutions cannot be readily contrived. However, past practice has shown that there are a number of sound ideas which—though they cannot always be guaranteed to work—are nevertheless worth attempting, if only on the basis of nothing ventured, nothing gained.

It is often helpful to make an initial evaluation of the situations which have just been described and to determine to what extent there really is a monopoly and the potential for its removal. For example, it will often be the case that an apparent monopoly exists because the sourcing has been inadequate or restricted to certain geographical or market sectors. Six factors may be considered:

- patents
- specification
- government restrictions
- intra-group trading
- 'locked-in' situations
- inadequate sourcing.

Patents

Perhaps the most difficult problem is posed by an enterprise possessing the patent, where the product is essential, and the search for substitutes or alternatives has proved fruitless.

A crucial first step is to establish the patent's expiry date. All patents have a finite life, a maximum of 20 years being the norm. Note that the holder pays an annual fee, otherwise the patent lapses. It is worth checking to ensure that the patent is still 'live'. If the product is important to the supplier there should be a corresponding awareness of this risk; however, mistakes have been known to occur on this count.

As the life of a patent draws to an end, the suppliers may become increasingly concerned about continued business when their unique position runs out; such anxieties may make them more amenable to improving the terms of trade well before the final date.

Specifications

Buyers should spend time and effort in gaining a full understanding of the reasons for any specification which has contributed to a monopoly situation. Many cases have arisen due to ignorance of suitable alternatives or from total lack of appreciation of the financial impact of such pre-selection blunders.

It is not uncommon for specification writers to be unaware of the commercial strictures innocently created by specifying a particular component or source by name. Buyers need to initiate discussions with specifiers so as to create the possibilities for flexibility and thus allow for increased competition. Such changes need to be approached with care and alternatives fully evaluated to ensure that they really will give the performance required.

The need for purchasers to be involved at the outset in the process of drafting specifications is essential (the reasons for this were set out in Chapter 9). It is at this stage that the purchaser is able to point out the cost incurred in using the specified item against the savings or other benefits, which can accrue if alternatives are permitted.

The common theme—of which the purchasing function has to take particular note—is that the ability of the alternatives to perform adequately is paramount and that there must be no substitutions without the prior approval of the users and specifiers.

Government restrictions

Government policy, or other considerations of a politically sensitive nature, create a further and potentially serious area of concern. Such factors usually stem from a broader macro economic viewpoint which attempts to use purchasing policy and purchasing decisions to achieve other social or political objectives. Such policies can range from the relatively benign, as illustrated by the UK Full and Fair Opportunity Policy (mid 1970s) with regard to the North Sea oil developments, to quite punitive ones, exemplified by conformity with the Arab countries' requirements for sourcing declarations and the consequent US Rubikoff Amendment.[1]

It is the nature of governments that these policies will change over time and the buyer must keep abreast of them. Trading practices, once actively discouraged, can quickly be restored to favour, and the reverse, as dictated by the shape of policy towards commerce and trade. Changes in the international situation can broaden the scope for obtaining competitive supplies and buyers must be constantly aware of these opportunities.

Experience has shown that innovative approaches to purchasing can result in considerably more freedom to trade being achieved than would otherwise have been considered possible. Government guidelines and even apparently restrictive legislation can be quite legitimately and legally circumvented.

Intra-group trading

Intra-group trading frequently restricts the buyer to obtaining goods or services from an associate or sister company and, as an acquisition policy, is common in large enterprises. However, it is not unusual to find situations where the buyer is in receipt of conflicting instructions or is subject to policies which are incompatible. Instructions to place orders with the most economic source conflict with those giving preference to the sister company.

Such conflict creates bad practice. Using the open market and the market information obtained to determine the price and then negotiating with the sister company, leads to hostility in the supply-market, where suppliers may decline to bid or put in high cover prices.

While no surprise need be expressed at companies ensuring that all their subsidiaries get as much in-house business as possible, this policy does not achieve mutually satisfactory results when attempted in combination with an approach based on competitive bidding.

These situations must surely reinforce arguments supporting the classic case for partnership relationships (discussed in Chapter 11). Buyers must move away from arm's length relationships to ones of close cooperation and synergy (described in Chapter 10). The suppliers need, in their turn, to change attitude, and start to regard the buying organization as a preferred customer and not something to exploit for its own profit motives. If the desired relationship cannot be established between companies ultimately having the same shareholders, then there is little prospect for the survival of similar arrangements where the common interests of joint stakeholders are not being served.

'Locked-in' situations

Instances are legion where the buyer lacks any operational flexibility due to precedents set by previous buying decisions aimed at securing continuity of supply. The purchase of spares, decisions to maintain commonality of equipment, or even the expense of getting a new supplier on a learning curve are common examples of tactical decisions taken to save short-term costs, but possibly without sufficient evaluation of the longer-term consequences likely to affect corporate profitability.

The best time to negotiate the purchase of spares support is prior to completion of the capital purchase itself. The supplier will be more disposed to make major concessions to achieve the sale of a capital item when engaged in the 'selling phase' of the interest cycle (described in

Chapter 9), notwithstanding the observation that the value of the contract for spares may exceed that of the main equipment over its life cycle.

The cost of changing suppliers will often be high. However, the price of retaining underperforming suppliers could be higher and have deeper and more profound implications. Suppliers who gradually become less competitive or whose products and services become outdated, could both share the untimely fate of the buying organization, in being driven out of business. Buyers need to take a strategic view of the supply-market and be fully aware of vulnerability from competing forces before embarking on any change in supply planning likely to have significant impact on future corporate competitiveness.

Inadequate sourcing

Of all the activities undertaken in the course of the purchasing process, supplier sourcing is probably the most critical. If buyers fail to identify the most productive, suitable, and imaginatively competitive sources, then the way to achieving the commercial outcome will remain barred.

As briefly mentioned earlier in this chapter, inadequate sourcing can create an apparent monopoly in the supply-market to all intents and purposes. Sourcing techniques may have been inadequate because the buyer failed to look at all the possibilities. Searches may have been restricted to the locality, the country, the region, or the continent, while not discounting the possibility of in-house provision, should such a capability exist.

Provided that the buyers are sufficiently well trained, they will look in less obvious areas, possibly nearer home or, alternatively, widen the search on a global scale. Any international approach entails being familiar with the relative costs of the logistics involved and the pricing structures of transportation rates—an area demanding expertise and current advice—but one which is being actively exploited by the multi-national companies (MNCs) in their drive to maintain market share. The effort devoted to widening the horizon can be justified only by the critical nature of the time or commodity. The total operation has to be cost-effective as there is a premium on the use of the scant resources in any purchasing department.

The common practice of seeking three quotes to determine competitive opportunity can be regarded as irrelevant only when the market is in a developing state, as the sample is far too small to be significant.

Furthermore, it indicates an attitude of uncritical conformity to orders without any conscious attempt to apply the appropriate management input which could demonstrate a positive result.

DEVELOPING SUPPLIERS

Even when there is truly a monopoly, the buyer has other options. One which has proved to be most effective is to develop suppliers to meet the buyer's needs, by persuading existing suppliers to expand or modify their range, or encouraging new ones to enter the market. Reference was made to this technique, **reverse marketing**, in Chapter 8.

In these situations the buyer will have to show the supplier clearly that there are commercial opportunities, benefits, and advantages from becoming involved in the new venture. It may be appropriate to provide assistance in the form of the following:

- The loan of experienced staff and the transmission of technical expertise.
- Financial assistance, by the injection of capital, soft loans, or direct purchase of tooling and dedicated machinery. Within this category consideration may be given to offering preferential payment terms to minimize working capital.
- The placing of long-term contracts thus allowing the supplier to amortize any investment over a reasonable period.

Training of management and other key personnel not only in the technology but also—in certain circumstances—in the general knowledge needed.

DOES IT MATTER?

A monopoly supply situation may not be totally disadvantageous. There are many instances where such situations are acknowledged to exist to the mutual satisfaction of both parties.

Taking the supply positioning model (described in Chapter 5), considerations over monopoly supply of low value items (strategic security) would focus on continuity of supply rather than price. Action by the buyer would be quite different had the item been categorized as being of high value (strategic critical).

Performance of supplier

Above all, the buyer may be influenced by the attitude and performance of the supplier. If the latter is helpful, productive, and innovative, then the trading arrangement may be quite satisfactory. It is the unproductive, inefficient, and exploitative monopoly suppliers that need to be tackled; the supplier preference evaluation technique (see Chapter 6) can be put to good use in providing buyers with an understanding of the suppliers' motives and anticipated behaviour in the future.

Vulnerability of supplier

The monopoly supplier may feel vulnerable, particularly if there are only a few customers, or one of these is particularly dominant. In an example which amply illustrates this contention, a monopoly supplier of a component for a product used in the retail trade had been behaving in an adversarial manner, which manifested itself in price increases well above inflation, as well as restrictions on delivery arrangements. The buyer took the initiative to set up temporarily importation of alternate supplies at an uneconomic price. When it became apparent that the supplier had no other use for the material—a by-product of other operations—apart from burning as fuel, then the perceived power balance between buyer and seller dramatically altered. As a result of the buyer's actions, a new trading relationship was established which included the necessary price stability and just-in-time delivery.

Strategies to redress the balance
If the supplier remains unwilling to reciprocate the buyer's concern, while enforcing a monopoly—as in the previous example—then the buyer can resort to a number of other strategies designed to lessen the problems, and if possible, redress the balance.

Buyers can:

- increase the information held about the supplier
- increase mutual dependency
- exploit the monopoly image
- cast doubt on the project viability
- separate the personal and business components
- make in-house
- implement forward buying
- form a buying consortium
- take over the supplier
- work on total costs
- seek mutually beneficial changes.

Increase the information held about the supplier

More than in any other circumstance it will repay buyers to have as much relevant information on their supplier as is possible. Visits to the supplier's sites are absolutely essential and they can yield a rich dividend in current information concerning for example, products, capacity, shop loading and finance.

This is an excellent area for the buyer to involve the services of the company's engineering and scientific staff. They may well be treated with less suspicion and, if properly primed, be able to ask questions which yield valuable commercial information and may include a detailed knowledge of the way in which products are made and services generated. A knowledge of the supplier's own sources and the prices being paid for component parts would be most useful when studying any justification advanced to support an increase in the price of goods or services.

Information on the general commercial situation enables the buyer to assess the vulnerability of the supplier, useful when pressure has to be exerted during tough negotiations. Finally, buyers need to have a proper understanding of the corporate structure of the supplying organization and the full extent of the transactions of the group with the buying organization. They may well find that although one particular supply item is a monopoly, the supplier has other business which is vulnerable to competition. Use of such factual information may well soften the supplier's stance.

Increase mutual dependency

Buyers can feel at a disadvantage when concluding that the extent of business they can place excites little response. Unless means can be found of determining the proportion of capacity taken up, or some yardstick on monetary value discovered, then this feeling of inadequacy may persist. Even with the established facts at the buyer's disposal, this does not itself guarantee any change in attitude when employed in subsequent negotiation because nothing may have been found out about the monopoly supplier's future investment plans. There may be an objective which sees the production line being phased out altogether in favour of a new process or a more attractive opportunity for profit-yield.

Possibly the imbalance can be redressed by placing more business with the monopoly supplier. In contrast to the base load, this business would be resourceable elsewhere and would have the effect of equalizing the relative bargaining strengths in subsequent negotiations. The supplier would now have to take account of the effect of the potential loss of this additional business if a satisfactory service in the monopoly situation were not to be guaranteed and the prospective additional order value lost elsewhere.

Exploit the monopoly image

Some monopolistic suppliers may be sensitive to bad publicity and embarrassed by their position possibly because of a fear that government authorities could take an interest and introduce regulations that would adversely affect their operation. Subtle reference to making the circumstances public may produce an acknowledgement which could be tactically advantageous in any subsequent negotiation.

Cast doubt on the project viability

The supplier may have cause to reconsider offering improved terms if the buyer indicates that further progress is being jeopardized by cost projections showing it to be uneconomic, as based upon the anticipated outlay against expected revenue on completion.

Buyers should adopt this stance only when justified by circumstances and with the full support of their technical users. Otherwise, the loss of credibility could have a disastrous effect on subsequent dealings.

Separate the personal and business components

Any transaction contains two dimensions, the business component and the personal component. The business component can be expressed as a continuum.

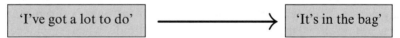

In a monopoly situation the seller can reasonably expect to have the business 'in the bag' but some of the ideas have been developed here to change this perception.

The personal component can also be represented as a continuum.

The buyer must try to keep the other party at the 'I want to help' end, and can do this by studying the seller as a person and determining how to exert influence to advantage. Often a personal appeal to the opposite party brings significant advantages.

Buyers should not be afraid to tell the supplier that they

- rely on their expertise
- trust them
- cannot manage without them.

It should always be remembered that it is people who do business, not companies, so it is sound commercial logic to keep the seller as a person on your side.

Make in-house

Nowadays it is rather against business trends to consider manufacturing in-house something that has previously been purchased from a third party. Nevertheless, for key **strategic critical** items it must be considered as an option when monopoly suppliers become exploitative. It is always useful to make the supplier aware that this remains a possibility.

Implement forward buying

When dealing with a product that is likely to rise in price in the future, then the option can be exercised to secure supplies at their present price levels, budgets permitting. However, the buyer needs to weigh the benefits carefully against the risks involved, which include adverse price movements, a change in demand or usage, the cost of holding stock, shelf-life, and obsolescence. Close liaison with other disciplines, particularly the marketing function, is essential to avoid the risk of overbuying.

Form a buying consortium

Some buyers seek to redress an imbalance of power by combining with other customers with similar requirements and approaching the supplier with the attraction of more significant volumes. Potential purchasers can expand their supply areas by the use of buying consortia. Whereas it may not be economic or practicable for one company to source from overseas, a consortium may make this an entirely feasible possibility. It is recognized that in some countries, particularly the USA, in certain circumstances a buying consortium would be considered illegal.

Take over the supplier

This is a somewhat extreme solution, and of course one which will be outside of the buyer's personal control. However, if the supplies are sufficiently important it is a course of action which cannot be ruled out.

Work on total costs

In most monopoly supply situations the price poses the most intractable problem. Unfortunately, buyers exclusively concentrate on this dimension at the expense of all other considerations. This could be attributed to the fact that fluctuations can be easily tracked. They often form the main element of performance measurement-data in any management information system (MIS).

Experienced professionals will be aware that major benefits will be derived by concentrating on the total cost of the acquisition rather than just on purchase price. Sellers seem to be more amenable to discussing total cost package and making concessions in order to secure the sale. Thus, significant improvements can be offered in the form of extended warranties, improved payment terms, and minimized maintenance and operation costs. These are just a few of the variables which might be considered. A more extended list is given in Fig. 12.1.

Buyers will find it most helpful to create a checklist such as this when approaching a major negotiation, particularly when dealing with a monopoly supplier.

Seek mutually beneficial changes

In pursuit of total value for money, buyers should be constantly searching for ideas that will take cost out of the process and so allow the supplier to provide items at a lower total cost without adversely affecting profit margin.

For example, it might be possible to set up an agreement to carry out IT maintenance in a way that minimizes the supplier's effort. Many computer systems are maintained by the supplier on a four-hour response time. If the first response can be met by arranging for the

Price stability	Installation
Price variation formulae	Commissioning
Payment terms	Manuals, etc.
Currency	Training
Delivery costs	Customization
Delivery location	Servicing
Insurance	Packaging
Performance guarantees	Returnable packaging
Promotional assistance	Risk sharing
Consignment stock	Exclusivity
Just-in-time delivery	Product endorsement
Maintenance	Surplus buy back
Spares	Toolkits

Fig. 12.1 Negotiating variables with monopoly suppliers

buyer's own technicians to change modular units then the supplier's frequency of visit will be reduced, thus producing cost savings for the supplier which can be passed on in the form of a reduction in charges, to the satisfaction of all concerned.

Cartels

In the context of this book, cartels may be defined as

Associations of suppliers working together to maintain or raise prices, or to divide markets between them and discourage unwelcome competitive activity to the point where it could be uneconomic and foolhardy to mount any challenge.

By their very nature, cartels are usually illegal, although not always so, and their status is affected by the policies of host nation governments. In the USA cartels are deemed illegal under the anti-trust legislation, which equally applies to both domestic and overseas trading of US-based companies. In the UK, such arrangements frequently come under the scrutiny of the Monopolies and Mergers Commission.

Cartels have been declared illegal within the European Union under the Treaty of Rome and there have been several well-publicized cases where companies have been heavily fined for operating them.

SIGNS INDICATING A POSSIBLE CARTEL

Since most cartels are illegal they shun publicity and this makes it difficult for the buyers to identify when one is operating. The buyer will need to be constantly on the alert in order to detect their existence. However, there are a number of signs that point to the **possibility** of a cartel being in operation:

- Prices moving strongly upwards inconsistent with inflation or other recognizable factors.
- The business always being won by the same supplier despite the fact that there would appear to be quite a lot of competition. Suspicions would be reinforced if other buying companies were experiencing the same thing but with a different supplier.
- Orders appearing to rotate on a regular basis between a small number of suppliers. Again, it would be worth checking to see if other buying organizations were experiencing similar situations.
- Suppliers exhibiting an uncommonly uniform inflexibility when negotiating over prices and commercial conditions despite the apparent existence of a competitive market.
- Price movement in unison.

None of these situations proves that a cartel exists but these indicators can serve as a warning to the alert buyer to that possibility.

EFFECTS OF BUYER BEHAVIOUR

A cartel can be effective only if there is trust between the members. 'Honour among thieves!' Without trust the cartel then collapses. Cartel members also need to understand fully the buying methods being used by customers and to be able to predict accurately the probable pattern of buyer behaviour.

Unfortunately, competitive bidding, one of the most commonly used purchasing techniques, is uniquely designed to provide participants with the information and comfort required to make the cartel succeed. The participants can readily inform each other about transactions of mutual interest. Indeed, it has been known for them to go as far as posting each other's bids. Obviously, any buyer using competitive bidding in this situation is vulnerable to the cartel's manipulation.

If the cartel thrives on sharing information, and buyer predictability, then it behoves the buyer to devise ways of placing limitations on information and becoming less predictable. Where possible an element of uncertainty should be sown in the minds of one or more of the cartel members. In this context, it should be noted that, whereas competitive tendering relies upon written documentation, face-to-face negotiation between two parties can be undertaken in private to the exclusion of third parties. It is inevitable that any transcript of the proceedings will omit certain nuances which could be essential to a total understanding of events which occurred.

IDENTIFYING THE WEAKEST CARTEL MEMBER

Buyers should strive to identify the weakest cartel member and suggest, for example, developing an innovative contract which provides commercial advantage. The aim should be to get the weak member to break ranks. In the event of this happening—the former cartel member may need the protection of longer-term contractual arrangements so as to compensate for the inevitable counter-measures to be expected from the remaining members.

For example, one company was buying large amounts of a packaging product, by placing annual contracts on the basis of competitive bidding. There were seven manufacturers of this product who had banded together to form a very effective cartel. Product prices had risen dramatically with no sign of slowing down. The buying company became concerned at the trends and undertook a study of the seven cartel members. Following enquiries they deduced that one company was in a rather weaker position than the rest. The buying organization undertook extensive negotiations with the weakest cartel member. In the end it persuaded the supplier to break ranks and offer a much better price in return for its entire packaging requirements. There was a consequent cost reduction of about 30 per cent. However, at the end of the contract period, certain managers within the buying organization wanted to go back to competitive bidding because they were of the opinion that the cartel had now been broken. The purchasing function maintained that it was necessary to continue with the same supplier over a period of years, provided prices remained competitive, as to do otherwise would expose their present supplier to retribution from other cartel members.

IMPORTANCE OF CONFIDENTIALITY

The terms of any negotiated agreement with a cartel member must be kept highly confidential within the buying organization and information should be disseminated only on 'a need to know' basis. If doubts are to be put into the minds of the cartel, it is vital that any records of bilateral negotiation are kept in the strictest confidence.

If a buyer fails to get cartel members to negotiate, then competitive bidding can be used to achieve the same effect, albeit at some extra cost. Supposing the buyer obtains five bids. Imagine the consternation felt within the cartel if the business was awarded to other than the lowest bidder and that the buyer steadfastly refused subsequently to discuss the basis for the decision with anyone. Would this not disturb the equanimity of the cartel?

REPACKAGING THE REQUIREMENTS

Another strategy—which has been used highly successfully in The Netherlands—is to repackage the enquiry so that no two suppliers will look at the same requirement. Supposing the project consists of elements 1, 2, 3, 4, and 5. Supplier A is asked to bid for elements 1, 2, and 3, Supplier B is asked for 2, 3, and 4, and so on. Experience has shown that this does create considerable confusion in the supply-market with a consequent decline in the cartel's effectiveness. Suppliers' bids tend to become uncoordinated and this provides an opportunity to negotiate all the elements with one or more suppliers.

Good use can be made of the total cost concept discussed earlier in this chapter. Cartels find it relatively easy to fix purchase prices but it is much more complicated to cover all other aspects and variables of a deal. It may therefore be possible to gain advantage in these other areas, notably those for example related to payment terms, warranties, allowances for rejects. In this way the supply price to the cartel is maintained and yet reduced to the buyer.

If the operation of a cartel has resulted in prices being raised beyond an unacceptable level, then strategies, such as those applied in reverse marketing, may well provide the means by which the supply price can be influenced to fall back to an acceptable trading level.

Summary

Monopoly and cartel situations need to be approached with considerable skill. The buyer must learn to be perceptive and innovative and—above all—has to be resolute when making an approach in such a distorted market.

Predictable and conventional methods of buying merely play into the hands of the supplier. The buyer must strive to find new angles, and in the case of cartels, create uncertainty. The adoption of a buying policy which entails so much risk—and responsibility—for the buyer must be in the full knowledge of the facts as presented to senior management and those with audit authority.

Unless purchasing initiatives in this most complex area of commerce receive the necessary support they have only a slim chance of withstanding the counter-measures which they will have to face from a well-organized and dominant supply base.

Notes and references

1 For many years the Arab countries required companies providing them with goods to declare that no part of the manufacture was Israeli based. In response the US Senate introduced an amendment to a trade bill making it illegal for US companies or their overseas affiliates to make any such declaration.

13

Organizing for impact

We have now completed the discussion on the strategic purchasing model. The development of theoretical models can be interesting but they are of little use unless they can be comprehensively and effectively applied in real-life business situations. This chapter will highlight some of the issues that arise as they are applied and suggest a plan for implementation, stressing the opportunities and pitfalls.

In Chapter 1 we pointed out that without a working operational purchasing strategy, it would be impossible to introduce upstream management and strategic purchasing into the purchasing process. The first step in any change programme must therefore be to put in place an effective purchasing strategy. However, in doing this it is critical to address issues and action in the correct sequence, otherwise a great deal of time, effort, and resources will be wasted and the overall results will be disappointing.

Enlightened companies realize that an empowered, involved, and entrepreneurial purchasing team, working in harmony with other functions in the organization, provides the key to retaining the competitive edge. This chapter presents considerations for the manager in deciding how best to organize to achieve high performance. But beware of the many purchasing managers who ask 'How best to organize?' Few will first address 'What are we trying to achieve?' If these two questions are not asked in the correct sequence, then there is a real danger of setting up a great organization which does not have any clear sense of direction.

The Parkin Wheel
The model that we have used for creating the correct sequence of action is described in what we call the Parkin Wheel; it is illustrated in simplified form in Fig. 13.1.[1]

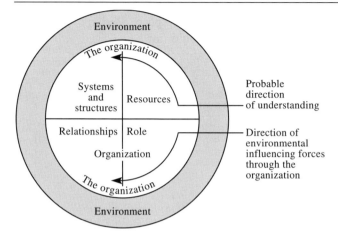

Fig. 13.1 The Parkin Wheel

When people enter a new organization, they normally learn about the job by going round the 'wheel' in an anti-clockwise direction. First, they gain an understanding of the **resources** available to them in terms of personnel, plant and equipment, finance, and so on. Second, they discover the **systems and structures** which are in place to allow them to do the job in an effective manner. For example, this might include how to get maintenance done, organize travel, or make a purchase.

As time goes on they start to build up a series of internal and external **relationships**. In many cases these will be informal rather than defined by the organizational structure. Such relationships will be numerous and many faceted and might include temporary alliances in order to perform a specific task or to perform as a long-term mentor. It is these relationships which enable the newcomers to perform their jobs in an effective manner.

Finally, and probably some considerable time later, newcomers will start to understand the role and purpose of the position which they now fill and to see how it relates to the broader environment both inside and outside the enterprise. When the true nature of the role becomes clear it may cause them to reconsider the type and extent of the systems, resources, and relationships that they need.

If the same sequence is followed when considering an organizational upgrade, then serious mistakes are possible. For example, if the first consideration is staffing (resources) then it is quite possible that the wrong numbers and type of personnel will be recruited. Or the enterprise may decide that it is running out of warehousing capacity and so identifies the need to build or lease more space. Perhaps storage is unnecessary in the first place, but this would not be realized until much later if the 'wheel' is implemented in an anti-clockwise direction.

In our experience of upgrading many purchasing organizations we have found that the most effective sequence is clockwise round the Parkin Wheel, that is, external environment, role, relationships, systems and structure, resources, although the sequence may require several iterations before a final consensus can be reached. Let us now look at what is involved in each of these stages.

External environment

No organization operates in isolation. The external environment provides both challenges and opportunities. Opportunities for success are maximized only if the organization responds appropriately to these stimuli.

As was the case with the 'organization' discussed earlier, understanding and influence may well be in opposition. Illustration of this point is made easier if by way of example we can visualize the different environmental aspects as forming a series of onion rings around the organization in the way shown in Fig. 13.2.

Before considering these layers it is worth noting that influence flows from the environment into the organization whereas understanding often has to start from looking outwards from within the organization.

Turning now to the layers themselves, those closest to the organization will tend to have immediate impact, will be readily recognizable, and be comparatively easy to understand and influence. An appropriate description of this layer would be **trading environment**. Key elements in this layer would be suppliers, customers, and competitors.

Environmental layers beyond the trading environment will tend to impact in a less immediate way, will not be so easy to recognize or identify, and will sometimes be difficult to either influence or understand. Some key elements of the next layer would be environmentalist, union, and media influences. An appropriate description of this layer would be **image environment**. A major point here is that, even though more difficult to understand than the trading environment, the power, impact, or influence on the organization of this image layer may well be very much greater.

The layer furthest from the organization is the one which we call the **macro environment**. Under this heading we refer to those elements which can have a massive impact on the organization, greater than either the image or trading environments. Because of their apparent lack of

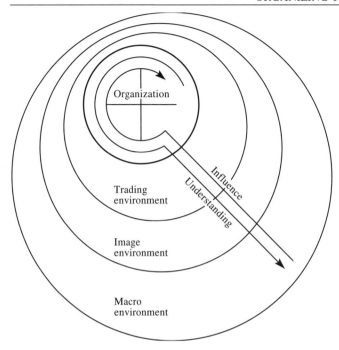

Fig. 13.2 The organization and the environment

immediate everyday impact or importance these elements may be given little, if any, priority. The nature of this layer is that it is often the most difficult to perceive, understand, forecast, and above all, influence.

Some of the key elements of this layer would be those effects created by technology, economics, demographics, culture, and politics. The technological element is probably the fastest moving of all. Its rate of change is exponential and could ultimately result in the extinction of one organization and the creation of another.

The subject of technology provides a striking example of our belief that there is a need to appreciate the subtleties of different elements of the environment. Here we have a force with potentially staggering impact which can often remain unnoticed when hidden in the minutiae of day-to-day tactical work. Political influence can place considerable restrictions on the manner in which any organization can operate. For example, UK public sector bodies are constrained by the need to demonstrate public accountability. Another example is the constraints on methods of purchase under the EU Procurement Directives and the anti-trust legislation of the USA. The response to these environmental elements should be to study and understand the legislation and to develop the most entrepreneurial approaches allowed by it rather than slavishly adhere to apparently inflexible regulations.

Role

The definition and understanding of the role of purchasing is a prerequisite of moving the function or process forward. An agreed **role statement**, endorsed at board level, will set the scene for understanding all that follows. This role statement must reflect both mission of the company and the commercial and cultural environment in which it operates. For example, it would be entirely inappropriate to have a purchasing role statement which places heavy emphasis on cost reduction when the company's priority is the introduction of new products on the fastest timescale possible.

PURCHASING GOALS

At the many seminars which we have run we often ask the apparently simple question 'What is the goal of purchasing?' We get an interesting variety of answers which themselves give insights into how the role is seen, both inside and outside the function.

Answers range as follows:

1 To manage the order-placement process as efficiently as possible.
2 To obtain goods and services of the right quality and price at the right time.
3 To reduce the costs of all purchased goods and services made on behalf of the company.
4 To provide the company with a competitive edge in the purchase of goods and services.
5 To manage the supply base so as to enable the company to maximize overall performance and competitiveness.

These five statements have been placed in the ascending order of strategic input.

Number 1 sees the process as very much a clerical function with the emphasis on efficiency.

Number 2 is service orientated with the emphasis on providing the user groups with what they want.

Number 3 identifies a specific but somewhat limited role of cost reduction. This is one of the most common positions, exemplified by an eminent former purchasing director who says 'You specify exactly what you wish to purchase and I will use all of our talents and skills to ensure that you obtain the best possible deal'. It has to be said that this view is both limited and flawed. It is limited because the purchasing process can provide a far wider contribution than price, as has been shown in earlier chapters. It is also flawed because by the time the specification has been completely developed many opportunities to obtain a competitive edge have been lost. This can come about only by multi-functional activities at the earliest possible stages of a purchase. Confining purchasing activity to the latter stages will limit opportunity.

Number 4 is an extension of the previous definition but in this case potential benefits can be much wider than just cost. Contained within the competitive edge are such benefits as quicker time to market, order of magnitude quality improvement, and enhanced financial arrangements.

Number 5 is the widest view of all, taking the line that the most important aspect is to manage the suppliers. This starts to bring the purchasing process into line with the broad concepts described earlier and with the implication of early supplier involvement.

CORPORATE GOALS

While the above options can reflect the difference in perception of the purchasing process as a range from the clerical/routine to the strategic/innovative, such definitions cannot exist by themselves. Any purchasing goal must reflect the goals of the entire organization. Chapter 11 highlighted the broad objectives that a company might have:

- cost leadership
- product differentiation
- market segment focus.

Any definition of the role of purchasing must have relevance to these corporate goals. Thus it is of little value to define purchasing as a means of cost reduction when the corporate thrust is on product differentiation.

ROLE STATEMENTS

Our recommendation is that, as one of the first actions of a restructuring programme, a role statement for purchasing is devised and endorsed by the board of directors and subsequently promulgated throughout the organization.

One of our preferred role statements is:

To achieve a significant and measurable competitive advantage for the company through the application of high quality purchasing processes including the management of key suppliers so that they are able to maximize their contribution to overall corporate goals.

Reference to 'significant' and 'measurable competitive advantage' moves the emphasis away from price alone to a wider field offering much more potential. It allows the role to be aligned with the broad corporate objectives outlined above. The statement also refers to a 'high quality purchasing process' which takes the focus outside of the purchasing function itself into the broader multi-functional area. Finally, it spotlights the valuable role that suppliers can play in meeting the purchasing organization's corporate goals.

SENIOR PURCHASING EXECUTIVE

We have used the title senior purchasing executive (SPE) to indicate the most senior person within an organization who has been given full-time authority and responsibility for the management of the purchasing process. Individuals may have titles such as purchasing director, vice-president purchasing, purchasing controller, or purchasing manager. In keeping with identifying the appropriate role for the function is the need to ensure that the SPE is positioned so as to be able to play a strategic role in the operation of the business. Otherwise the entire purchasing process will lack a professional approach, be involved too late in the procurement cycle, and have insufficient representation at corporate level.

Ideally, the SPE will report directly at board level and have a major influence in business product and project development. Whether or not the SPE has direct-line commitment authority will depend on the nature and stage of development of the organization.

AUTHORITIES

There are two discrete schedules of authority related to the purchasing activities. These are expenditure authority and purchasing authority.

Expenditure authority

This is the authority vested in the budget holders enabling them to incur costs which will be allocated to the cost centre (revenue or capital) for which they have responsibility. For any purchase, the expenditure authority rests with the client (budget holder) subject of course to overall constraints set by the board of directors. In taking decisions to incur expenditure, budget holders must ensure that they have been delegated the appropriate authority by the board. Under this schedule there is no authority to sign or issue purchase orders or make contract commitments with third parties (including in-group sources) on the company's behalf.

Purchasing authority

This is the authority to place an order or contract on suppliers. All purchasing authority is vested by the board in the SPE, who may formally re-delegate limited authority to members of staff both inside and outside of the purchasing departments. Individuals are not permitted to make commitments unless the SPE has previously delegated them specific authority to do so.

It is, however, important to note that no purchasing commitment can be made without prior expenditure authority.

Organizations should ensure that these different lines of authority are clearly defined and understood by all concerned. This will add clarity to the entire purchasing process.

Relationships

When the role issues have been resolved and the role statement has been agreed and established, it is then possible to turn attention to the way in which the purchasing process will be organized within the company. In particular it will be necessary to define the scope of responsibility and the role of purchasing professionals *vis-à-vis* those in other functions, recognizing that the purchasing process requires the interaction of many individuals and areas.

THE SCOPE OF RESPONSIBILITY

The value-adding/market-managing role for purchasing involves much more than just buying. 'Buying' covers the mechanical process of turning a requirements list into an order (although in the retail world the term describes a higher status activity involving product selection, supplier selection, and pricing for purchase and sale). Buyers' instructions usually come from clients or requisitioners (increasingly being termed 'internal customers' as the total quality culture takes hold) or from a computer-based inventory management or MRP (materials requirements planning) system.

Previous chapters have shown that purchasing's responsibilities are wider and include influencing the specification process, innovative sourcing, and managing supplier performance after awarding the order. More than just 'placing the order', purchasing is uniquely placed to rethink the approach to the market and is delegated the authority to

- commit to legal contracts with suppliers
- manage the company's interface with the supply-market.

This means not only developing and maintaining access to interested and high-performing supply sources, but also orchestrating the different contacts at all levels which the company has with suppliers, thereby influencing their expectations of needs and what they think they can price at to meet them.

The responsibility span stretches wider with the **materials management** concept. Alongside purchasing, there are two other management umbrellas: **materials control** (the definition of materials usage-requirements and purchase schedules to meet manufacturing plans) and **inventory management**, in a physical sense (storing and moving stock) and also the application of stock accounting and stock optimization techniques.

The choice of responsibility-span depends on the manager's objectives.

- A focus on **buying** will improve control of the order-placement process; regularize who has authority to place orders; ensure that proper terms and conditions apply, and that transactions are properly recorded, for various purposes. **The theme is 'reaction to need'.**
- A focus on **purchasing** will build on this by optimizing specifications and lead times (through close collaboration with users); will get best supplier responses in terms of initial costs and subsequent performance; and through acute commercial awareness will manage the risks to the company due to its considerable financial exposure to the supply-market. **The theme is 'close management of an external resource upon which the business critically depends'.**
- A focus on **materials management** will reduce costs in the supply chain by ensuring coordination between the different disciplines involved. **The theme is 'minimizing costs by close coordination of related activities'.**

Previously stated arguments which say that purchasing should be part of materials management rest on the premise that the different disciplines that make up materials management do not, if left to themselves, optimize the whole. If the functions are brought together then more impact can be made on reducing costs in the supply chain. This is a legitimate objective but it already begins to make the assumption that purchasing is simply a cost element in the overall chain. The danger is that purchasing's increasingly important contribution, that of securing access to the sources to which the supply chain is connected, is eclipsed by an over-emphasis on operational task based efficiency.

The span could get even wider. Current trends might encourage the manager to think in terms of a **logistics function**, taking all of what is in materials management and adding things at the other end of the business such as external distribution of products and identifying the require-ments of the external customer. Logistics does have its own unique role to play but if it (wrongly) is seen as primarily being about achieving cost reduction through coordination then the chances of perceiving purchas-ing's role as supplier manager become exceedingly slim.

Of course, all organizational groupings can work well if the unique contribution of each component function is constantly recognized, but the evidence is that such clarity of purpose does not exist in many organizations; hence our argument (also put in Chapter 1) that pur-chasing should exist as a discrete entity on the input side of business, just as sales and marketing stimulate demand for and manage the output. The rest of this chapter therefore focuses on organizing a purchasing function in line with our core beliefs. A further aspect of scope concerns the extent to which professional purchasing is applied to the entire requirements portfolio. In Chapter 1 we pointed out that professional purchasing should be applied to all acquisitions. However, this may be easier said than done.

Lamming and Dooley have shown that substantial numbers of buyers feel that they are not qualified to purchase such items as plant/machinery, computers, machine tools, contract staffing, automobiles, and aircraft.[2] Furthermore, Lamming and Dooley have shown that only 40 per cent of purchasing departments surveyed were involved in the acquisition of capital equipment, and only 27 per cent for computer hardware and software. Very similar figures were obtained for a whole host of other categories. While these figures must be treated with some caution because of the skew of the sample towards manufacturing and the public sector, our own investigations would support the broad conclusion.

Any company seeking competitive advantage through enhanced pur-chasing processes must set its sights on applying the best practices to all acquisitions. As we concluded in Chapter 1, this includes capital purchases, computing requirements, advertising, travel, to name but a few. This means that organizations must take care to describe and get agreement to the scope of operations at the very outset.

Whatever the scope of the activity, it will be important for all parties to agree the role that is to be played by the purchasing professionals, whether they are located within or outside of a dedicated purchasing function. Professional purchasing input must start at the supply planning stage and continue throughout the procurement cycle. All parties need to understand and fully support this by deeds as well as words.

CROSS-FUNCTIONAL TEAMS

As we have shown, the purchasing process starts at a very early point in time, often prior to a specific need or opportunity being identified. Throughout the process there is a need for many individuals and functions to be involved at various times if the outcome is to offer maximum benefit to the buying organization. Prime responsibility for the process also moves between functions as shown in Fig. 13.3.

No	Stage	Responsibility Prime	Assist
1	User identifies need	User	—
2	Requisition and specification	User	Purchasing
3	Acquisition planning	Purchasing	User
4	Requisition approval	User	—
5	Develop bid slate	Purchasing	User
6	Enquiries/screening	Purchasing	User
7	Develop commercial terms	Purchasing	User
8	Tenders/tender evaluation	Purchasing	User
9	Contract award	Purchasing	—
10	Expediting	User	Purchasing
11	Handling changes and claims	Purchasing	User
12	Confirm services received	User	—
13	Authorization for payment	Accounts	—
14	Warehouse and inventory management	User	Purchasing
15	Authority to declare surplus	User	Purchasing
16	Disposal of surplus	Purchasing	User

Fig. 13.3 Functional involvement in the purchasing process

This table is for guidance only and it is expected that all parties will cooperate and coordinate closely with each other at all stages of the procurement process.

Systems and structures

With relationships defined, the organization can now turn its attention to the systems and structures which are to be employed. By far the most important of these are policies and procedures and the structure of the organization itself.

POLICIES

It is surprising that many organizations have no clearly defined policies for the guidance of those that undertake the purchasing activities. Others have a large tome which is a mixture of policies and procedures in an almost unreadable form. In these organizations these policies are often honoured in the breach rather than the compliance or else ignored altogether. It is certain that such policies are not known about or understood by anyone outside of the purchasing function.

In our experience the most effective approach is to create a slimline pocketbook of about 20 pages which sets out those purchasing policies that are mandatory. The document serves as a reference for all those involved in purchasing on behalf of the organization. If the document is printed in an attractive and professional manner and then given wide distribution it will be read by many who would otherwise not know how the purchasing process operates and what rules govern it. This in itself can act as a catalyst for greater interfunctional understanding and hence cooperation.

The policies manual would include

- an introductory page signed by the chief executive
- the purchasing role statement
- a chart similar to that shown in Fig. 13.3
- organization of purchasing activity
- delegation of authorities schedule for expenditure and commitment
- procurement methods and their general applicability
- relationships with suppliers
- relationships with other companies within the group
- reciprocal trading policy
- reference to the use of the buyer's terms and conditions
- personal ethical standards.

MODEL PROCEDURES

To provide further guidance to all, the policies manual would be supplemented by a set of model purchasing procedures covering the most commonly encountered purchasing situations. All such procedures would be compliant with the policies and serve to eliminate the need for individuals to devise procedures from first principles every time. However, they would not in themselves be mandatory. Staff would be encouraged to use them for common situations (thus ensuring policies compliance) or alternatively, to set up a specific procedure to meet a special case. In this latter circumstance it would be mandatory to ensure that any such procedure was set up in such a way as to comply fully with the purchasing policies.

Purchasing procedures will differ, depending on where the purchase falls within the supply positioning model, but will include a very simple system for handling low value purchases whether they are undertaken by purchasing staff or others outside of the function. A minimum requirement would be a means of recording the transaction and identifying who had carried it out and when.

Since many staff could be involved in making low value purchases it would be desirable to provide them with some simple, easily understood guidelines within which to operate. This is best achieved by the provision of a very simple (two page) guide setting out what has to be done and recorded. Some organizations now issue this guideline in the form of a small plastic card which fits easily into the pocket.

ORGANIZATION

Companies who see purchasing as a primary business function endow one person, the SPE, with unlimited authority to commit them. This goes alongside the authorities vested in other functions to requisition (i.e. to approve a 'need') as discussed previously in this chapter. Commitment can thus be seen as 'arranging for a need to be satisfied'.

However, the SPE, having won this authority from the board, must accept total accountability for the quality and effectiveness of all purchasing actions, whether or not taken by 'professional' buyers.

This reiterates the point made earlier that the purchasing process, in all but the smallest companies, requires the involvement of more than one person. Commitment authority has to be delegated to skilled purchasing professionals and, in the best companies, also to non-purchasing personnel on a carefully controlled basis.

In a large company, purchasing may take place within different operating units on the same site, or at different sites within one country or across several. A hierarchical approach is needed. Purchasing activity may take place at one or more of the levels shown in Fig. 13.4.

Centralized	Full-time professional purchasers; central location
Decentralized	Full-time purchasers with line responsibility through to the purchasing director, based at a works or country location
Local	Based at a works location and directly responsible to the local general manager, whether full or part time on purchasing, is recognized as being the local focus for purchasing action; dotted-line functional responsibility to purchasing director
User buyers	Full time on other work—e.g. production, research, sales, etc.—but authorized to make or initiate day-to-day purchases of a routine nature to help the job along. This may involve direct order placement or 'calling off' requirements from a supply contract already set up by purchasing

Fig. 13.4 A buying hierarchy

Despite this hierarchy, no matter how extensive the delegation away from the centre, the SPE remains totally responsible for all purchasing activity.

However, given the current trend towards establishing autonomous self-running business units within a large conglomerate, the SPE may instead be accountable to the main board for 'functional excellence' as distinct from specific commitment decisions. For example, in several major organizations the SPE has no authority to make commitments with suppliers but has full and unlimited authority to monitor, evaluate, and change the operation, standards, and personnel who do make the commitment.

Either way, effective delegation creates the need for a clear sense of overall purpose, unambiguous but flexible procedures, authority levels set to correspond to buyer skill-level and the supply exposure, and appropriate systems for feedback and control.

But what are some of the considerations which guide the SPE in deciding how much to keep at the centre and how much to delegate?

CENTRALIZATION AND DECENTRALIZATION

Points of the pendulum?

'We can get a bigger discount by centralizing our purchasing and combining volumes' or 'our overhead costs are too high; we can reduce them by disbanding central purchasing and let our individual operating locations handle it themselves'. Which option has your vote? The chances are that you can be in a company and hear the first phrase one year, and four years later in the same company hear the second. Such is the ebb and flow about how best to organize the purchasing team.

When might centralization make sense?

In some companies, centralizing might be the first step along the road towards creating purchasing excellence. Focusing the reporting of expenditure at a central point allows a total cost picture to be built up, possibly for the first time. From the centre can come policy creation and guidelines, tiers of authority delegation, feedback mechanisms reporting key expenditures, local content monitoring, and purchasing performance measurement.

Centralized structures are also appropriate when purchasing activity has been fragmented around the company with many local agreements set up to buy the 'same' things, often unknowingly from the same suppliers. There may be cost and discount incentives by doing 'bigger' deals or alternatively it may be appropriate to share the order with more than one supplier to avoid over-dependence on one source for strategic critical supplies.

Creation of 'call-off' or 'umbrella contracts' can also save time for buyers, releasing them from tactical firefighting activity and allow them to focus on more strategic issues. Bringing in a major computerized purchasing system or the introduction of fundamental changes in policy or practices are again examples of strategies best led from the centre, as is the need to demonstrate the re-establishment of control in the wake of a major supplier fraud or abuse of delegated authority.

In the centralized model the theme is 'Action at the Centre', as Fig. 13.5 shows. But, just supposing the centralized approach slows things down and creates client hostility? Being decentralized may have advantages after all.

Decentralization: a better option?

Decentralization may be the better option, but it depends on the desired management strategy for purchasing at the time in question. If major changes are not envisaged company-wide then purchasing can focus on optimizing rather than changing its impact. Perhaps it is desirable to

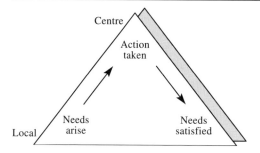

Fig. 13.5   The centralized approach

speed up purchasing's response, better to satisfy the needs of local end-users or internal customers, or to increase visibility in order to be involved earlier at the time when the needed materials or services are being specified.

Maybe it is time for the buyer to break into the close liaisons that salespeople love to develop with designers and local specialists, liaisons which work so much in the supplier's favour, often without their 'prospect' ever suspecting that they are being targeted and conditioned to behave as the supplier wants them to.

In a widespread company or one composed of independent business units, local needs can perhaps best be satisfied by local deals. To bring in the heavy artillery of central purchasing power is not appropriate. With decentralization, the theme is 'Purchasing Action at the Working Interface', as Fig.13.6 illustrates.

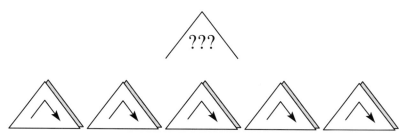

Fig. 13.6   Decentralized response to need

But what do the people at the centre do, if there are any left? Indeed, is there a role for 'the centre'? Suppose that a supplier starts playing off one operating location against the other, or a local buyer becomes too dependent on or 'loyal towards' one local supplier and fails to recognize more competitive alternatives from further away? Or different buyers in different locations start adopting ad-hoc approaches that make the company look fragmented and unprofessional (possibly even undesirable) to its suppliers? Maybe, after all, it would be better to go back to a centralized approach.

And so the pendulum swings to and fro in the search for the best organization. It is important to recognize that both approaches can succeed at meeting objectives for which one or the other organization is best suited. But when the time comes for change, significant reorganization is involved. So is there a 'best' which harnesses the benefits of both options? We believe that the 'CLAN' holds the answer.

THE CALL OF THE 'CLAN': A CENTRE-LED ACTION NETWORK

A Centre-Led Action Network (CLAN) approach can be used by organizations with widespread activities taking place with a high level of local autonomy. The locations may all be within one country or spread across many. There are several fundamental differences between the centralized and CLAN approaches, a key one being to distinguish between the centre's 'doing' of purchasing activity, and 'championing' it.

In CLANs, purchasing action stays at the local level but buyers do not act in isolation because they are kept connected directly with each other by a very small team at the centre, the network managers. The latter stimulate contacts between buyers with similar problems, but based at different locations, to get together to plan concerted action. If a call-off contract is set up then the buyers support and use it, since they created it, not someone remote in central purchasing. Buyers now know who their counterparts are around the company, so they can get in touch with those who will have the latest market intelligence on issue A, or whoever has just done a deal with supplier B and on what terms.

Back at the centre, strategies are initiated for developing the purchasing professionals in networking, training, career development, sponsoring network conferences, and so on. Above all, the purchasing director is the champion for purchasing: setting the standards for functional excellence, promoting the function within the company as a whole, ensuring the company's image and purchasing power is not fragmented in the supplier's eyes, and being held accountable by the chief executive for purchasing's overall performance and contribution to the business.

The mnemonic 'CLAN' captures how the centre relates to local activity—a Centre-Led Action Network. The aim of the centre team is to create an overall environment within which local purchasing actions can be successful, measuring success against standards which represent true functional excellence. Figure 13.7 illustrates this.

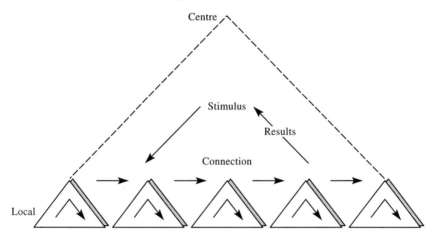

Fig. 13.7   The Call of the CLAN

CLANs successfully avoid the problems arising from the rigidity of the central approach, because it is purchasing professionals at the locations who

- do the actual purchasing
- are accountable to local general management for satisfying their internal-customer needs in a commercially astute way (i.e. they deliver the results)
- manage and develop the local purchasing team members
- collaborate with local internal customers and suppliers
- link with purchasing colleagues from other locations if appropriate to share market intelligence, or to create a 'group' contract
- give selective feedback to the centre.

While eliminating the problems of centralization, CLANs at the same time avoid the fragmentation of decentralized alternatives, because it is the centre which

- sets the standards for functional excellence, and the policies and controls which guide and coordinate all local purchasing actions, and ensures compliance
- reinforces belief in, and demonstrates the effectiveness of, the function at the centre of the company and across the different business lines and other functions

- provides a sounding board and sponsorship for actions planned by local purchasing managers
- leads strategies for change (these may be external strategies for the supply-market or with particular supplies, or internal strategies designed to enhance the effectiveness of the function)
- provides access to resources—e.g. training, information, technology— and maybe some direct participants for key tasks
- stimulates selective synergy between different sites.

This is illustrated in Fig. 13.8.

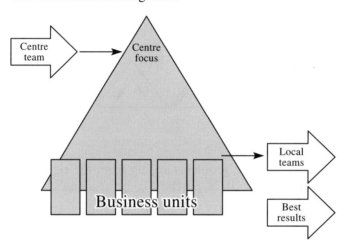

Fig. 13.8 CLAN

As an organizational model for purchasing, CLAN exists in its own right. Conceptually it is quite different from the centralized and decentralized approaches and most certainly is not a compromise between them. For many organizations it provides tomorrow's solutions to today's problems. It is important to note that CLAN is a sophisticated model and works only if there is, at the heart of the company, a clearly understood and supported mission for purchasing and—throughout the network—a sound infrastructure of management control, effective delegation, and accountability for task. In a company where purchasing has been fragmented, or maybe not even recognized until now as a discrete business function, it may first be necessary to go through a phase of centralization to establish the direction and policy framework within which to delegate in future.

THE CALL OF THE CLAN IN TOMORROW'S BUSINESS

Today's 'blue chip' companies, and those who are developing to become the 'blue chip' companies of tomorrow, sustain their success by continually trying to improve their effectiveness. Being satisfied with the 'status quo' is an anathema. Companies want to be lean, flexible, and responsive; CLANs are. Company cultures are changing to the view that truly excellent results are achieved through people, not in spite of them. This is the CLAN culture.

Large conglomerates are breaking up into autonomous business units to encourage entrepreneurial, measurable, profit generation. CLANs solve the riddle of how to do this without losing purchasing power or a key stake in the supply-market. In some companies the signs are that the once-young local business units are putting on the 'weight' of middle-aged organizational growth. CLANs help slim companies to stay that way. Above all, they succeed in positioning the purchasing function as a strategic activity managing the supply base upon which businesses increasingly depend. They are concerned with managing real risks, trading real money, and delivering real results.

One multi-national company goes still further in seeing the creation of the CLAN as the key to the success of the total business, not just purchasing. In its Pacific region, where company operations are growing dramatically and stretch across some 14 countries and many thousands of kilometres, the chief executive perceives the purchasing function as the one discipline which has direct interface with all the other functions making up the company. His complete support for the 'gathering of the CLAN' is driven by the belief that the creation of a high-performing purchasing team not only will deliver profitability but also, more profoundly, will be the catalyst that achieves high performance throughout the company.

The 'Call of the CLAN' in today's business appears to be a loud one!
SYSTEMS!

COMPUTERIZATION

The objectives of introducing computer systems into the purchasing process are threefold :

- To eliminate low skilled and routine clerical work associated with the creation, collation, and retrieval of records and other data. This would include all documentation associated with requisitions, purchase orders, contracts, goods received notes and invoices.

- To provide several different groups with a means of keeping track of activities such as the progress of orders through the system.
- To collate data and thus generate information which can be used in deciding purchasing action or developing strategic purchasing initiatives. This could include data concerning previous prices paid, quality problems with suppliers, or impending major difficulties.

It is not the purpose of this book to provide detailed guidance on the selection and implementation of such a system. However, we give below some fundamental suggestions which, if followed, will eliminate many of the common difficulties that are encountered:

- Be very clear on what you expect to gain from the installation of any system. Tailor the specification to meet your true needs and avoid too many 'nice to haves'. Ensure that ease of use or user friendliness are paramount in the specification. Do not accept systems that are complicated or difficult to use.
- If at all possible, avoid the temptation to opt for a 'bespoke' system because the packages do not appear to meet all of your needs. Bespoke developments can cost many times the original budget and take over twice as long as anticipated to bring to fruition. They are then very costly to keep up-to-date. It is better to accept a package which is an 80 per cent fit rather than design your own 'ideal' system.
- Do not accept a purchasing system which is an 'add on' to an accounting or MRP system. When this happens the system will often be inflexible and inadequate for the needs of a modern purchasing process. It will fail to generate the controls and information which are needed to perform at the highest levels.
- Do not change the core of a package solution. Make changes by adding interfaces. Do not try to incorporate too many 'special' features at the outset as these will greatly increase the cost and possibly destabilize the product. It may be better to modify in-company procedures to fit the computer software.
- Provide dedicated project management resource to all stages, from design through implementation.

All purchasing staff should be provided with computer terminals with access to the system and also access to wordprocessing, spreadsheets, and database management. The use of these is essential in undertaking purchasing at its highest level.

Resources

With structures and systems defined, it is now possible to turn our attention to the required resources. For purchasing, this will be mainly human resources and the way in which they are managed.

QUALITY OF STAFF

The quality of purchasing staff must match the role and requirements of the function. Thus, if the role is defined in high-level strategic terms, it will be necessary to staff the function with individuals who are capable of undertaking work of that quality. In any case, the levels of education and training of the purchasing staff must be at least equal to the levels found in other parts of the organization. If the calibre of staff in purchasing is not equivalent to that of staff in marketing, production, or finance, then purchasing may be discounted and other functions may be reluctant to involve purchasing in key strategic decisions because of the perceived lack of intellectual power.

At some stage it will be necessary to make a serious evaluation of the incumbent staff in order to determine whether they are going to be suitable for their newly perceived roles. A major consideration when upgrading the purchasing function is an assessment of the likely new demands which will be made on personnel. These must be described in terms of the new roles performed at the highest levels. The temptation to restate the content of the old-style jobs must be avoided at all costs.

Analysis of these demands will provide an indication of the number and nature of the job positions. From the resulting job descriptions, pictures of typical effective incumbents can be drawn. Predictions of future successful job performance can be listed in terms of relevant standards of key competencies and personality characteristics.

Effective selection decisions depend on arriving at accurate and informed perceptions about employees and potential employees based on these criteria. For this analysis to be fair and objective, interviews need to be structured and undertaken by trained personnel. In addition the use of occupational tests, questionnaires, and exercises which elicit job-related behaviour will offer the best opportunity to maximize objectivity.[3]

This process will enable management to assess existing staff in terms of suitability to the newly created positions and including any training and development needs.

When the overall assessments are complete it may be necessary for the management to make some hard decisions about the future of the existing employees. Management may consider that some members of staff (for a variety of reasons) are not going to be able to fit in with the skills and requirements of the new structures, even though training is offered. However, in order to comply with legal requirements and to maintain morale, every effort should be made to ensure that those who have no future in the upgraded function are treated in a considerate and positive manner. Unsympathetic treatment will damage morale of even those who are destined to remain within the organization.

RECRUITMENT

The analysis of current staff may indicate the need to recruit others from outside of the function, or indeed, the company. The same rigorous assessments should be applied to all candidates. Recruiters should not rely solely on interviews but should seek to gain as much other information as possible through the use of occupational tests, etc.

PROMOTION

Some companies are now using these techniques to evaluate the potential for promotion. The argument here is that current performance gives information only on the ability to do the existing job but gives no real evidence of how the individual would perform in a different role.

It is important to be able to demonstrate that the purchasing function does offer promotion opportunities and is not the 'end of the road' for a career. Ideally there should be a flow of high quality staff into the function and moving on to higher levels in other parts of the organization. In addition, certain highly qualified, high-performing individuals should be given assignments of greater responsibility accompanied by promotion to a higher grade. This move should be based on performance and not length of service.

CULTURE

Finally in this area we should consider the culture within which purchasing staff are required to work. The best results arise from a culture of trust and empowerment where individuals are not constrained by bureaucratic rules and regulations. This should be reflected in the amount of freedom which is given to enable individuals to act as business people rather than clerical factotums.

Summary

Here is an action checklist in desired sequence for those contemplating a change to their purchasing organization.

1 Create and publish a purchasing role statement. Ensure full management support and advocacy. Although creation must be the first task, it may be preferable to delay the promotion and publication until some time later when some capability has been introduced into the function. Publicizing too early raises expectations which will not be met unless the new organization is ready. Failure to respond in a positive and effective manner could damage credibility and set back the entire change programme.
2 Define role of and appoint the senior purchasing executive.
3 Define and agree scope of operation; get agreement of all parties.
4 Create and publish a slimline purchasing policies manual including a description of authority schedules. Publish this at the same time as the role statement.
5 Write a set of model purchasing procedures.
6 Set up a purchasing system for low value items.
7 Write and publish a user buyer's guide.
8 Agree the organizational structure.
9 Define staff requirements in terms of quantity and quality.
10 Assess current staff and make decisions on their future involvement.
11 Recruit staff as required.
12 Set up and implement targeted training programmes.
13 Introduce strategic purchasing concepts.
14 Foster cross-functional team activities.

Notes and references

1 This model was developed by J. N. Parkin and in turn was based on an idea suggested by R. C . Williams.
2 These data are taken from a Survey of Non-traditional Purchasing of Goods and Services prepared by R. C. Lamming and K. Dooley of Bath University, September 1994. This conference paper had not been formally published at the time this book went to press.
3 Detailed information and advice about occupational tests can be obtained from the addresses listed below.

British Psychological Society
St. Andrews House
48 Princess Road East
Leicester LE1 7DR
Tel. 0116 549568

Institute of Personnnel Management
IPM House,
Camp Road
Wimbledon
London SW19 4UX
Tel. 0181 946 9100

Details of some of the main texts in this area now follow.

Cronbach, L. J. (1984) *Essentials of Psychological testing*. Fourth edition, Harper and Row, London.
Holdsworth, R. F. (1972) 'Personnel selection testing—a guide for managers'. British Institute of Management, London.
Saville, P. (1985) 'Psychological testing and personnel selection,' *John Tyzack Review*, September 1985.

14

Measurement, audit, and benchmarking

Why measure?

Of all the questions posed to consultants by both purchasing professionals and others, the one which is most frequently asked is 'How can we measure the performance of the function?' It is of course a most difficult one to answer. Before attempting to provide some guidance in this area, it may be appropriate to try to decide why measurement is deemed to be necessary in any case.

> *'You cannot control what you cannot measure and you cannot measure what you cannot understand.'*

The lack of understanding of the true nature and potential of the function is at the root of the difficulty. At the same time the absence of a high-profile, easily understood, form of measurement often makes it impossible to gain the attention of senior management who are concerned with other problems and priorities.

This perhaps explains why so many purchasing departments receive little senior management attention and end up failing to perform the 'right tasks in the right way'.

Control is essential for the efficient management of a function. It becomes essential therefore to create some forms of measurement which will assist and facilitate that control, and provide management with means of monitoring progress.

One further point, held by some professionals, is that the measurement process can itself be used to promote the function to senior management—a form of image-building. There is undoubtedly some truth in this, but great care must be exercised in the way it is performed as it could be interpreted as a way of seeking self-glorification.

WHAT IS SO SPECIAL ABOUT MEASURING PURCHASING?

We have shown that there are three key processes within a business which will contribute to corporate performance and profitability: sales, production/operation, and purchasing. When it comes to measurement there is a substantial contrast between purchasing and the sales and production/operation processes of a company, both of which have a much firmer basis on which to assess themselves.

Production can relate its performance to the amount of manufacturing output and the cost required to achieve it. It can monitor machine downtime and capacity utilization, together with non-financial factors such as safety and environmental impact. In non-manufacturing and indeed non-profit-making organizations, output can usually be measured in terms of the level and extent of service provided or the number of customers serviced compared to related costs.

Sales performance can be measured either against volume sold, or by the more recent technique of key account management (see Chapter 6). Whichever method is used, it is possible to calculate the price of manufacture of goods to be sold so that the difference between this and the sales realization, less the selling costs, becomes the profit contribution. Movements in profit contribution become the basis for measurement of performance at both the individual and organization level.

The problem with attempting something similar for purchasing is that there is no firm cost figure which can be used as a base. It is all very well to say that without professional purchasing the cost would have been increased by £n000, but it is impossible to prove the claim. This is why the attempts to treat the purchasing function as a form of profit-centre have been doomed to failure. In any case, good purchasing—as we have seen—is not just about price, but embraces many other complex factors.

Faced with this dilemma, managements have retreated to measurements of headcount and simple, if misguided, efficiency statistics which often mislead and do nothing to provide an understanding of what is really happening. As a result it is common to see quite the wrong course of action being taken.

Over the years many leading authorities have attempted to provide solutions to this dilemma, but always with only partial success. This chapter will not provide an amazing revelation but it will suggest some alternative approaches which it is hoped that the reader will find useful.

WHAT ARE WE TRYING TO PROVE?

The purpose of measurement is threefold:

- to provide a basis for effective control
- to provide stewardship of resources
- to demonstrate to others the benefits of the purchasing process playing a strategic role in the business.

In a sense what we measure, and how we measure it, will depend on which of the above three purposes we are trying to address. Thus measurements to facilitate stewardship of resources would be concerned with staffing and cost and their relation to the output of the operation. To demonstrate purchasing's strategic role support, data would be directed at showing where the function has had a key impact on the overall operation in terms of profit or other performance. Note that providing a basis for effective centres still remains the most difficult factor to address.

WHO WANTS TO KNOW?

In a similar vein, the measurement may relate to the audience for which it is intended. For example, the production department will judge the purchasing function by availability of production materials and so the number and frequency of stockouts would be an important measurement for them. In contrast, the engineering department might be much more concerned with quality and so would make a judgement based on the number of defects and rejects. The finance director's priority could be cashflow and the contribution to the bottom line profit.

In responding to these varying requirements the purchasing manager might decide to measure everything. The result is likely to be a mountain of statistical data which no one reads, let alone understands.

We would suggest that the types of measurements of the purchasing process will depend on how it is currently perceived by senior management, and by others, and the stage in development being sought. In response, purchasing should report on the data that support the perception while, at the same time, stimulating interest in information which supports a higher level approach to the function.

The six-stage process

Reporting could be in one of six stages.

Stage 1 If purchasing is seen as an unnecessary function, then the message to be imparted is one of 'standards and control'. Data should be produced to demonstrate the extent of expenditure being made in the supply-market and the lack of control in making purchases. It should be possible to demonstrate that the absence of contractual safeguards further creates vulnerability to financial exposure.

Stage 2 If purchasing is seen as the regulator of the order-placement service, then data should be provided to show the efficiency with which the process is being undertaken. However, additional information/data should be produced to demonstrate that there is potential for a significantly greater contribution in the area of price and cost savings.

Stage 3 If purchasing is seen as being concerned about realizing the lowest price, then demonstration of real achievements in this area will be an important factor in the continued renewal of a licence to operate. Where the same items are purchased from year to year, this can be done by means of deviations from standard costs but in other situations it will be necessary to report on a 'case by case' basis picking up only the most significant. Additional data should be provided to demonstrate that total lifetime cost is more important than price and that other non-price factors such as delivery, payment terms, and warrantees can make a significant contribution to profit.

Stage 4 If purchasing is looked at in terms of profit contribution then data to support total cost performance should be supplied. It is now important to demonstrate how purchasing can influence corporate performance in other ways. It is crucial that the supply base has sufficient suppliers with the capability and willingness to provide the buying organization with a competitive edge. Factors of vital concern extend to maximizing supplier performance and contribution, and to contracting so as to ensure that the company is protected in the event of shortages, supplier failures, or excessive cost increases.

Stage 5 If purchasing performance is associated with achieving a wide range of specific results then there has to be a system of regularly reporting actions which have had a significant impact. It is now time to think in terms of linking the purchasing process to overall corporate strategy and consider such matters as market growth, penetration of new markets, the rapid introduction of new products, and cash management.

Stage 6 If purchasing is seen as a key strategic contributor then specific measurement may not be needed. Attention should now be focused on purchasing as a primary business process rather than as a functional activity.

By use of this stepwise process it becomes possible to focus on achievements which can be directly related to the appropriate audience who will be expected to renew the licence to operate while at the same time raising awareness and expectations in further developments.

Operational or strategic?

The stepwise approach shows that what is measured will also be heavily influenced by whether purchasing is considered by senior executives to be merely an operational/administrative activity or, alternatively, a key strategic resource. It shows that, as the balance shifts towards strategic, the emphasis on measurement will change from readily discernible data (such as the number of orders or the total value) to more intangible concepts (such as the number of monopoly supply situations eliminated). In fact, in one international company which has placed purchasing at the top of its internal agenda, the managing director has made it clear that only a strategic overview, without 'supportive data', is required.

Consideration of the operational-vs-strategic approach suggests that the supply positioning model (described in Chapter 5) could be used in helping with the 'measurement dilemma'. We have already shown that purchases can be divided into at least four quadrants. In turn their associated prime purchasing objectives will suggest different forms of measurements. This theme will be developed later.

The use of indicators

In the end, however, in our view, there is no one absolute measure of purchasing performance, even when analysis is confined to one of the supply positioning segments. Within any one segment there are likely to be at least two or three forms of measurements (indicators) which must be taken together and carefully interpreted. This will disappoint those seeking a simple unified measure but this finding represents our best advice.

Even with the use of indicators, great care is needed with their interpretation. As an example, let us suppose that we wish to measure the level of activity within a purchasing department. At first glance we might conclude that the number of orders per month per buyer would be a useful indicator. And so it would be—except that orders require differing amounts of effort. A capital purchase costing £50 000 will obviously take more time than an order for £150 of stationery.

This gets worse when we start to take account of efficiency measures. Let us suppose that a buyer decides to create a blanket order (one order) to replace a yearly total of 240 orders (averaging 20 per month). In the first month the number of orders per buyer has reduced by 19, and it could be interpreted that the buyer had become less productive. This would be misleading. In a full year the number of orders that the buyer handles reduces from the nominal 240 to just one, making a mockery of the statistic if taken in isolation. The consolidation into one order enables the buyer to expand work capacity and the number of orders will again be increased but this measurement continues to successfully conceal the productivity element.

Similarly, by itself, the number of stockouts is meaningless. This parameter has to be read in conjunction with the number of stocked items, the value of inventory, stock turnover, the nature of the business being evaluated and crucially, the number of times there was a requirement for an out-of-stock item.

A final point on the use of indicators. They can be used to compare only very similar operations or trends within any one business but if used carefully, they can be a powerful motivating influence to the purchasing team.

Overall indicators

The use of supply positioning can be of substantial assistance because it segments the supplies, suppliers, and the supply-market. Before considering each of the segments in turn, it would be appropriate to identify three indicators which could apply to the entire operation. We have called these significance, involvement, and upstream/downstream balance.

SIGNIFICANCE

Significance relates total revenue expenditure of goods and services, to revenue for a profit-making organization, and to total costs for a non-profit organization. Significance is expressed as a percentage of revenue or total costs. In truth, it is less a measure of performance and more of a way of demonstrating the significance of bought-in goods and services to the organization concerned.

As already explained, significance is now reaching a level of 55–65 per cent for most manufacturing organizations, and even higher in certain high-tech industries. In service industries, the level will be between 25 and 40 per cent of revenue, and in the public sector areas it will be a similar level of total costs.

Significance does not usually include expenditure on capital items, which are an equally important part of purchasing's remit. It is desirable to quote this as an additional explanatory note.

INVOLVEMENT

Involvement may be defined as the percentage by value of bought-in goods and services which are subject to a professional purchasing process. To qualify for inclusion in these figures, goods and services must be acquired with the full participation—not just the placement of orders—of purchasing or by some other group with delegated authority from the senior purchasing executive.

A figure of 95 per cent or above would indicate that purchasing is truly fulfilling its mission. A lower figure would give the signal to management to examine the reasons. We have seen that it is quite common to find that certain specialist areas such as advertising, research, and transportation have jealously guarded their prerogatives and excluded themselves.

An annual monitoring of progress against this indicator would provide management with an overview of whether purchasing was beginning to play an increasingly strategic role in the business. It might also be illuminating to plot this same involvement figure for each of the four supply positioning segments in order to show whether purchasing was involved in key activity or just trivia.

UPSTREAM/DOWNSTREAM BALANCE

Upstream/downstream balance (UDB) relates to the concepts set out in Chapter 3. Total personnel associated with purchasing is allocated between upstream and downstream activities. UDB is the percentage of total staff engaged in upstream activities. An increasing percentage trend would indicate that the purchasing function is concentrating on the more productive areas and consequently is making a greater contribution to corporate profitability.

Indicators related to supply positioning

In order to select other appropriate indicators, it is timely to reiterate the purchasing goals associated with the four quadrants (see Chapter 5), shown in Figs 14.1, 14.2, 14.3 and 14.4.

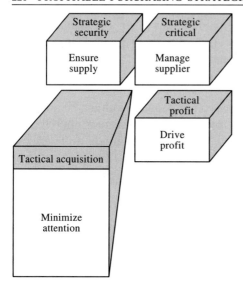

Fig. 14.1 Supply positioning and purchasing goals: tactical acquisition

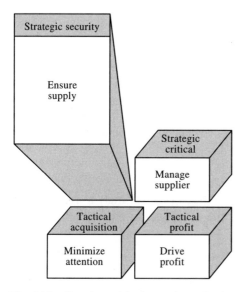

Fig. 14.2 Supply positioning and purchasing goals: strategic security

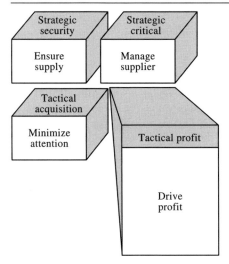

Fig. 14.3   Supply positioning and purchasing goals: tactical profit

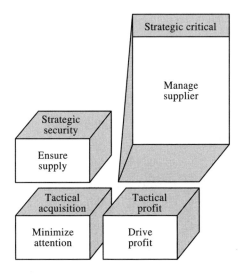

Fig. 14.4   Supply positioning and purchasing goals: strategic critical

Taking the four categories in the usual order we may draw the following conclusions.

TACTICAL ACQUISITION

The purchasing objectives for items classed as tactical acquisition are to minimize effort and resource and to delegate action back to the user as far as possible. Overall corporate effort can be minimized by the setting up of blanket orders and contracts, reducing the number of sources, being less concerned about price but seeking a high level of service to minimize the buying organization's administration.

Performance measures

Performance measures will therefore be related to the efficiency with which the function is performed. Indicators will include the extent of blanket order coverage, expenditure per buyer, the numbers of suppliers, and the number and levels of service contracts. Overall success will be measured by the ability to reduce the level of activity.

Specific indicators

Specific indicators which have proven to be very useful in the tactical acquisition sector are

- operating costs as percentage of spend
- percentage value of blanket order coverage
- spend per buyer
- speed of requisition turnaround
- reduction in the number of suppliers
- numbers of orders delegated to user functions
- frequency of systems buying contracts
- number of suppliers on EDI.

In this area it will be possible to make inter-company comparisons but trends will be equally important.

STRATEGIC SECURITY

In the strategic security area the most important objective is to ensure security of supply, consistent with the demands on quality, reliability, and environmental (Q/R/E) impact. Purchasing priorities are directed towards improving Q/R/E and seeking ways of improving security of supply.

Performance measures

In this sector performance measures will be related to stockout frequency, the level of rejects due to quality problems, the introduction of new sources or alternative (more easily resourced) products, and the availability of contingency plans should supply be threatened.

Specific indicators

Specific indicators for use in the strategic security sector are

- number of new sources identified
- number of alternative products identified
- amount of reduction in the quality reject level
- number (percentage) of stockouts
- number of items moved out of this quadrant.

TACTICAL PROFIT

It has already been shown that tactical profit items are the main source of profit contribution for a buying organization. The purchasing objectives will, accordingly, be directed towards maximizing that contribution by professional operation in the marketplace.

Performance measures

It is in this sector that performance measurement will focus on 'savings' or cost avoidance. In a manufacturing environment it may be possible to use the 'standard costing' system whereby purchasing are set cost targets based on the previous year's actual performance and any improvement taken as a contribution to profit. Unfortunately in periods of high inflation the figures become blurred, especially when 'inflation factors' are built in to the base case.

In a non-manufacturing environment it is even more difficult. The only known satisfactory method is to compute savings on a 'case by case' basis where purchasing has used an innovative approach to secure additional benefit. Such calculations will exclude any benefits arising from competitive bidding or volume discounts from list prices when the levels are predetermined by the seller. Care should also be exercised when making claims or benefits arising from resisting price increases although each organization should develop its own policy in this area.

Specific indicators

Specific indicators relating to the tactical profit sector include

- cost reduction by identification of new supplier
- cost reduction by substitution of a purchased product or service
- cost reduction by new logistics initiatives
- negotiated purchase price reductions
- negotiated improvements in total cost of operation
- cost reduction by post-tender negotiation (requires care)
- value of negotiated additional benefits
- value derived from improvements in payment terms
- improved warranties and other terms of trade
- cost benefit of reduced stockholding.

STRATEGIC CRITICAL

The final sector is strategic critical, where we encounter purchasing objectives which are a combination of ensuring security of supply and getting best value for money. Unlike strategic security, it is not possible to achieve security of supply without regard to cost, since, by definition, these items represent a large proportion of total spend. In turn this means that it is very important to manage all aspects of the supplier's operation.

Performance measures

Performance measurement in this sector will be mainly concerned with demonstrating the reduction of risk at the same time as obtaining increased value for money.

Specific indicators

Specific indicators for the strategic critical sector would include many of those listed for tactical profit and in addition:

- elimination of monopoly supply situations
- negotiation of mutually beneficial improvements with suppliers
- improved supplier performance with regard to quality and reliability
- number of recognized innovations
- number of contingency plans/update frequency.

Limitations of indicators

A review of this list of indicators and a comparison of them with other factors which purchasing professionals must take into account reveals that there are many aspects of the contribution made by the function which are not adequately covered. Among these are

- reducing risk exposure by negotiating tighter contracts
- changing specification and design to provide easier market access
- developing innovative contract strategies
- anticipating supply problems and taking action to overcome them
- identifying cartels and taking action taken to circumvent them
- adding substantial value by negotiating total cost improvements such as insurance against failure, training, etc.
- improving supplier and market information including medium/long-term prices and availability forecasts
- upgrading supplier performance by working on its organization
- reducing stockholding by the use of consignment or imprest stocks
- minimizing risks from currency fluctuations
- contributing to 'make or buy' decisions.

Many of these factors cannot be readily subjected to detailed numerical assessment. Indeed, some of them may be regarded as being qualitative rather than quantitative. It would seem then that some other method of evaluation is required in addition to the indicators in order to provide managements with an overall measurement of purchasing performance.

Management by objectives

Having reviewed and worked with all of the possibilities, we have concluded that some form of management by objectives, supported by appropriate indicators, represents an alternative approach to the measurement of the function. These can be backed up by relevant selected indicators.

To be really effective the objectives should be concisely and clearly written and supported by detailed measurable plans. An example of a successful format is given in Fig. 14.5.

Objective	Specific support plan	Timing criteria	Success
Develop a new strategy for the purchase of steel products on the international markets.	1 Review and classify all company steel purchases.	March	List ready
	2 Identify all major international suppliers, visit, and discuss.	May	List ready Visits completed
	3 Evaluate alternative procurement strategies.	June	Presented
	4 Test on major purchase.	September	30% improvement
	5 Write report and propose future action.	November	Issued

Fig. 14.5 Example of purchasing objectives

In this example the outcomes of the specific plans are quantifiable and measurable (success criteria) and can be used as part of a quarterly or annual report. Senior management should be involved in the setting and agreeing of the objectives in the first instance and can then use them to monitor the progress of the function through the ensuing periods.

Most of these objectives should relate to upstream activities. At this stage purchasing activity should be at its peak of investigatory, imaginative, and intellectual endeavour. Concentration on these upstream concepts will ensure that the overall direction of the function is correctly focused.

Measurement summary

Measurement of the purchasing function will never be an easy matter. Whatever data are collected will require careful and expert interpretation. Purchasing management should develop an understanding of the purpose of the measurement and for whom the results are intended. They should then make a careful selection using a mixture of indicators and more qualitative objectives.

In the early stages the focus will be on maximizing efficiency and demonstrating financial advantage to the budget. Next will come simple measures to demonstrate tangible financial benefits and awaken interest at senior level.

Later will come wider and sharper measures designed to increase the focus on effectiveness. The intention here is to sustain and encourage the motivation of senior management to continue the change process and to stimulate awareness of the potential supplier's contribution to business goals.

These measures will be increasingly comprehensive and sophisticated and move the organization towards the evaluation of business relationships and high quality processes.

Benchmarking

It may be true to say that purchasing will have reached maturity when it no longer becomes necessary to have it measured in order to prove its worth. In those companies where purchasing is regarded as a truly strategic function, no such measurement takes place. However, the purchasing contribution is evaluated in terms of the manner in which it manages the supply base to maximize contribution to the organization.

Many organizations are now starting to use the benchmarking concept as a method of measuring the performance of their entire range of activities. The basis of the technique is to define **best practice** of the process involved by comparison with other organizations carrying out similar activities. Plans are then developed to introduce changes which bring the organization into line with best practice. The assumption is that if best practice is being followed, then the results will be the best that can be achieved.

We have developed a benchmarking technique for purchasing, the basis of which is to define best purchasing practice, derive a method of quantitative measurement of it, create a numerical scale for comparison, and then to rate organizations against the scale. The result is that company management, including those not entirely familiar with purchasing concepts, are presented with a numerical representation of how their own organization compares with 'best in class'. In turn this gives an indication of what and how much needs to be done to be able to operate on a par with the best, in order to improve performance.

This method of evaluation is not specific to one industry or type of purchasing and so comparisons can be drawn across the widest number and range of companies and business sectors. This is of special importance for those companies working in the business sectors which have less well developed purchasing activities because it then enables them to see what is being achieved in other fields.

Some companies are now using the benchmarking process to track progress as they move through a period of change in the purchasing function. It can also be used to compare performance between operations in different parts of the same company.

The best practices profile

The key to the benchmarking approach is the definition of purchasing best practice. It is obvious that if this is not correctly defined then any comparative evaluation would be worthless. For this reason we have developed a best purchasing practices profile which describes the best practices either now in use or being considered by the most forward-looking organizations. This profile will include the results of research undertaken by certain universities and the concepts and observations being developed and implemented by ourselves for our leading clients.

In considering what purchasing processes make up best practice it is important to have a clear understanding of the difference between purchasing strategy and strategic purchasing. As we showed in Chapter 1, these are terms which are used interchangeably when discussing the purchasing profession. For convenience we repeat our definition of these terms.

PURCHASING STRATEGY

Purchasing strategy is concerned with identifying, selecting, and implementing an overall change programme designed to place the purchasing process at the heart of a business so that it is able to make the maximum contribution to corporate profitability and the gaining of a commercial competitive edge. Among other factors, it encompasses defining the mission of the purchasing function, the framework within which to work, and the type of organization and staff to be employed. It is the foundation on which strategic purchasing is based.

STRATEGIC PURCHASING

Strategic purchasing is the development of ways of approaching and interacting with the supply-market, taking account of not only the present situation but also how it might be in the future. It is based on the belief that buyers can determine and change the supply-market within which they function. Strategic purchasing cannot be applied to the market as a whole but only to specific situations within it.

Benchmarking starts with identifying the building blocks of purchasing strategy and defining them for use as the basis of comparison of the buying organizations included in any study sample. It then goes on to examine the techniques which should form part of an effective strategic purchasing operation.

Building blocks: purchasing strategy

The six factors or building blocks which form the basis for an effective purchasing strategy (see Chapter 2) can now be developed into a numerical scale against which individual operations can be measured.

For each of these building blocks we have described the practices in poor or immature organizations (score 1–3), in organizations either undergoing development or partially developed (score 3–5), and in the world-class leaders in the field (score 5–7). It thus becomes possible to match the organization being evaluated against these scales and to show how it is currently performing against each of the six building blocks. Adding together the scores of each building block results in an aggregate which indicates overall performance and comparative position.

The six building blocks (described in more detail in Chapter 2) which make up the purchasing strategy profile are

- contribution and influence
- purchasing and audit framework
- organization
- relationships (internal and external)
- systems
- staffing and training.

CONTRIBUTION AND INFLUENCE

No matter how expert the purchasing personnel or how effective their procurement methods, there will be little real positive impact on the business unless the purchasing function is in a position to make a high-level contribution and can have a strategic influence on the conduct of the business.

In this building block we evaluate where the purchasing function stands in the business and whether it is in a position to exert influence. We consider seniority of the key personnel, their contribution to strategic decisions, the extent of cross-functional teamworking, the authority structures, the level of involvement with the entire purchasing portfolio, and the measurement methods applied to the purchasing function.

PURCHASING AND AUDIT FRAMEWORK

In many organizations there is either little proper control of the purchasing process, or it is strangled by bureaucracy and unworkable regulations which stifle initiative and good purchasing practice.

In this building block we evaluate the regulatory framework within which the purchasing process is performed. We examine the existence of a mission or role statement, the nature of policy and procedure manuals, the flexibility in approach, the extent to which buyers are empowered or restricted, the existence or otherwise of adequate controls, and the relationship with the internal audit function.

ORGANIZATION

The organizational framework within which the purchasing function operates can have a profound effect on its effectiveness and its relationships with key clients. Underlying the organizational issues is the dichotomy relating to centralization and decentralization.

In this building block we evaluate the nature of the organization, paying particular attention to the centralization/decentralization issue and the levels of internal hierarchy. We seek evidence of networking between buyers and buying organizations and the methods used to balance and allocate workloads. We also examine the balance between 'upstream' and 'downstream' activity and identify whether failure-related functions are still performed.

RELATIONSHIPS (INTERNAL AND EXTERNAL)

Purchasing can no longer be considered an isolated function, working at arm's length from suppliers and internal clients alike. The best operations work closely with all parties in the supply chain to achieve an overall goal of achieving a competitive edge for the buying organization.

In this building block we examine the nature of the relationship with the internal clients, looking for evidence of procurement involvement early in the procurement cycle, the effective operation of multi-functional teams, and the effective management of the buying organization's contacts with suppliers.

We also examine the relationship with suppliers, starting with whether the organization has developed and is using any means of differentiating between the various types of relationships which are required. We look for evidence of the application of strategies specific to a supplier or group of suppliers, as opposed to a uniform approach to the supply-market.

For certain key products we look for evidence of supplier involvement in design and development and of a joint approach to enhancements in quality, delivery, and service, together with significant reductions in total cost. We also evaluate the techniques used for measuring and enhancing supplier performance.

SYSTEMS

Computerized systems offer organizations the opportunity to dramatically increase the information on which to base decisions and a means of eliminating routine administrative activity. To be fully effective, organizations must ensure that the needs of the business drive the systems design and operation and not vice versa.

In this building block we look for evidence of the effective use of computerized purchasing systems which eliminate routine clerical activity and provide buyers with real-time information which can be effectively used to make supply decisions. We evaluate whether the computer systems truly meet the needs of the purchasing organization or whether they have been provided without too much thought to future development.

We also examine whether EDI links have been established with key suppliers and the extent to which these links enhance or inhibit purchasing performance.

STAFFING AND TRAINING

No purchasing operation can be effective unless it is staffed with high quality professionals who are continually updating and enhancing their knowledge and skills and can promote the function within their own organization.

In this building block we examine the levels of education of purchasing staff and compare them with those of staff in other functions, consider movement of staff in and out of the purchasing function, and evaluate the nature and effectiveness of training programmes.

Building blocks: strategic purchasing

The second part of the benchmarking exercise is concerned with the techniques and tools which contribute to effective strategic purchasing. In this area we search for evidence of the understanding and implementation of a variety of techniques, many of which have been described earlier in this book. Again, the organization is scored on a scale of 1 to 7 for each technique. In addition we look for evidence of an overall integration of these techniques into one strategy.

The techniques which will be considered are:

- supply positioning or portfolio analysis
- vulnerability analysis
- supplier preference analysis
- procurement marketing

- reverse marketing
- vendor improvement programmes
- competitive advantage analysis
- cost modelling
- risk management.

At the end of this benchmarking exercise the company will have a very clear idea of how it compares with the best and what it needs to do to improve its operation. In each of these categories the scoring system would be as follows:

1 Technique unknown and unused.
2 Technique known but never fully understood or applied.
3 Received training in the technique but do not regularly apply it.
4 Experimented with the technique but with little success.
5 Technique applied in one or two instances with some success.
6 Technique applied in a number of areas with some success.
7 Technique used regularly and routinely with substantial and identifiable success.

Summary
We said earlier in this chapter that there were no 'amazing revelations' to unfold. However, we have shown that organizations can use a variety of techniques depending on their own particular situation. Whichever route is chosen, it is important to communicate the underlying rationale of the methodology, and to provide a means of readily interpreting results, to all levels of management.

Index

Added value, (*see also* Corporate
    profitability), 4–7
Audit, framework for purchasing, 16–19,
    229–230

Benchmarking, (*see also* Vendor
    improvement) examples of benchmark
    factors, 227–232
Best practice:
    as a comparative process, 227
    in building blocks of purchasing strategy,
    14
Bought-out materials and services:
    as a percentage of sales, (*see also* Sales),
    101, 174
Buyer(s):
    attitude to buyer–supplier relationships
    (*see also* Pilling, Bruce and Zhang),
    138–139
    initiatives to realize goals, 120–121
    positioning in capital project team, 3

Centralization and decentralization, 201–204
Centre-Led Action Network (CLAN),
    204–207
Chartered Institute of Purchasing and Supply
    (CIPS), 3
    Survey of poor performance of
    subcontractors (1993), 3–4
Competitiveness:
    contribution possibly by purchasing, 7
Competitive advantage assessment, 150–151
Competitive edge:
    through harmony with other functions, 188
    through identifying vulnerabilities, 87–89
    through vendor rating and improvements,
    111–116
Competitive tendering:
    drawback to bidding as a process for
    selecting partners, 165
    in the approach to cartels, 185
Computers (*see also* Systems), personal
    computers (PCs), 23
Contract box, 157–158
Contracting out:
    proportion and extent of, 8

Contract strategy:
    finalizing the contract, 37
    purpose of, 34–35
Contribution and influence:
    purchasing and its impact, 15–16, 229
Conventional appraisal, 36
Corporate goals, 193
    (*see also* Declared partnership goals)
Corporate profitability:
    (*see also* Added value) creation, lowest
    acquisition cost, 4
    options to obtain it, 8–11
Cost analysis perspective, 134–135
Cost improvement, (*see also* Purchasing),
    118–120
Cross-functional teams, 198–199

Declared partnership goals, 155–156
Downstream activities:
    management, scope and function of, (*see
    also* Upstream/Downstream balance),
    27

Electronic data interchange (EDI), 22–23
Enabling foundation:
    redirection of procurement resources to
    maximum effect, 26
    relationship with the integral building
    blocks, 24–25
Ethics:
    as a policy issue, 17
    entertainment and gifts, 127
European Union (EU):
    as a factor in the macro-environment, 191
    influence of directives on procurement
    practice, 141

Government purchasing:
    public accountability, 191
    restricted flexibility, 174

Information technology (IT), (*see also*
    Systems), 22
Innovation:
    rapidity of, 139–140
    rate of technical change, 88

233